MATHIAS GOCIK

Touch His Wounds

Easter Daily Scripture Reflections

First edition

ISBN: 9798315590774

This book was professionally typeset on Reedsy.
Find out more at reedsy.com

To my dear Grandma Maria,
who from my early childhood
was instrumental in forming my faith in God
and whose unfailing faith in the Risen Christ
always shone for me as a beacon of hope.
I am forever grateful.

May the Risen Christ welcome you into his love
so that you may rejoice forever before the face of God.

Contents

Preface

In the Greek Catholic tradition, the prayer hymn *O light gladsome* expresses the everlasting joy that springs from the resurrection of Christ. This prayer hymn recalls the deep faith of the Christians in Jerusalem from the 2nd century. As a symbol of the resurrected and glorious Christ, a perpetually burning lamp was placed into his empty tomb. This hymn was sung as a candle was lit from this burning lamp and brought out of the tomb ceremoniously to remind everyone that the joy of the resurrection never ends. The resurrected Christ now shines for all to see and brings everlasting joy to everyone that follows him!

In addition to our own personal prayers before opening Holy Scripture and reading God's Word, let us also pray this powerful hymn and so prepare our hearts to receive God's graces:

O Light gladsome
of the holy glory of the Immortal Father,
the Heavenly, the Holy, the Blessed, O Jesus Christ,
having come upon the setting of the sun,
having seen the light of the evening,
We praise the Father, the Son, and the Holy Spirit: God.
Worthy it is at all times to praise Thee in joyful voices,
O Son of God, Giver of Life, for which the world glorifies Thee.
Amen.

Like the women or the soldiers?

Easter Monday,
April 21

Today's readings:
First Reading: Acts 2: 14, 22-33
Responsorial Psalm: Psalms 16: 1-2a and 5, 7-8, 9-10, 11
Alleluia: Psalms 118: 24
Gospel: Matthew 28: 8-15

In my previous book, the devotional "Lent: Daily Scripture Reflections", the meditation from yesterday (Easter Sunday) demonstrated that the empty tomb of Christ is not proof of his resurrection. To this day the tomb is empty, Christ is not there, but even still, the empty tomb is not taken as proof of the resurrection. The only proof of the resurrection is any person who had a living and personal encounter with the resurrected Lord Jesus Christ and now bears witness to Him. In today's Gospel we see such encounters. We have two groups before us, two very different groups, who encountered the Risen Christ. We have the first group, the women, and then the second group, the soldiers, specifically those that were guarding the tomb.

Several things distinguish these two groups from each other.

They are images of our society and images of us all, so let's try to classify ourselves, according to the following differences, into which group we belong.

The first group are the women at the tomb, who we know very well from the Gospel. These women know Christ, they followed him, they met him during their lives, they listened to his words. Among them are also those women who lived in all sorts of sins, but after meeting Christ, they changed. They allowed him to enter their lives and transform their hearts from stone to hearts of flesh, full of love and sacrifice. Meetings with Christ, before his resurrection, changed them radically. We belong to this group, if our meetings with Christ also change us for the better. Regarding the second group, we cannot say that they did not know anything about Christ. Everyone in Jerusalem knew very well what happened with Jesus, even the Gospel confirms this in several places. The very fact that a cohort of soldiers (600 soldiers) went to capture him on Thursday evening in the garden, testifies that the Romans, as well as the Jews, were very afraid of Jesus and his disciples and went with so many soldiers because they thought that a rebellion would occur. The soldiers who subsequently guarded him while he lay in the tomb, may have belonged to these soldiers who captured him. Nonetheless, they definitely knew him, met him, saw him, at least at Christ's trial and during his passion. Meetings with Christ, before the resurrection, did not change these soldiers. We belong to this group, if our meetings with Christ do not even move us. Christ says one thing and we do another. These are those who, by their lifestyle - although they know Christ and know who he is - still ignore him and say they don't need him. We could say that this is a pretty popular group even today.

Subsequently, Christ rises from the dead and emerges ceremoniously and gloriously from the tomb. We do not know how it happened, nor when it happened, we only know that it was sometime between sunset and dawn. The verses before today's Gospel describe angels who rolled away the stone and sat on it - and at that moment, Christ is no longer in the tomb. Both the women and the soldiers saw this event. Immediately after, the resurrected Christ himself appears in their midst and says *"Hail!"* This is the solemn and glorious greeting of a victor - very strong words and even stronger here because they are directly spoken by the Risen Lord. And here again we see the differences in these two groups. The women, when they look at Christ, they rejoice and bow down to him in adoration. We belong to this group when we also come to Christ and fall on our knees before him, asking him for his blessings. On the other hand, in the fourth verse, (which is not part of today's Gospel) it is written that the soldiers froze with fear and became like dead men. We belong to this group when holy things paralyze us, when we believe they have no meaning for them, when we say we do not need them. In those moments, we also are like dead men.

The last thing that distinguishes these groups is their mission. The women receive a mission from Christ to announce the Resurrection to the apostles who were hiding in fear and to encourage them to go to Galilee and there await their meeting with Him. We belong to this group when we also bring Easter joy to all people, especially those around us and spread the peace and life of Christ. The soldiers also received a mission, but it was from the high priests to spread the message – which was exactly the opposite of what they saw – that the body of Christ had been stolen by the disciples while they were sleeping. The soldiers are sent to spread lies. We belong to this group when we also ignore the truth about Jesus, when we think we can manage life without him and we are not interested in getting involved in the life of the Church. In addition, knowing the truth and ignoring it, is a very grave sin, in truth it is the sin of Satan. It is the greatest stupidity we can do in life - knowing the truth, knowing Christ and throwing him away, ignoring him, because coming to Christ is no longer fashionable, interesting, or according to us necessary.

So which group do we belong to? Our life testifies to which group we belong to. If we found ourselves in the group with the holy women who allowed themselves to be changed by Christ, let us continue in this good work, but if we found ourselves in the group with the soldiers, it is time for renewal, it is time to change, it is time to accept the Truth into our lives, specifically the risen Christ, to restore what was broken and revive what was dead. Christ is our life and our hope, let us not turn our backs on him but accept him with joy so that we too may live a new life.

Why are you weeping?

Easter Tuesday,
April 22

Today's readings:
First Reading: Acts 2: 36-41
Responsorial Psalm: Psalms 33: 4-5, 18-19, 20 and 22
Alleluia: Psalms 118: 24
Gospel: John 20: 11-18

Suffering, sadness, pain - it is all part of life. Often we ask, why suffer this pain, why struggle with this situation, why endure this difficulty, why did God allow this? We often look for solutions, but we don't always have the answers. But that is okay, because it is precisely in this kind of situation, in despair, darkness and pain that Jesus Christ enters into our lives, He who is alive and glorified. When one experiences this powerful meeting, it becomes clear that there really is no peace or comfort apart from the risen Jesus Christ.

Today we see it in the Gospel, Jesus asks Mary: *"Woman, why are you weeping? Whom do you seek?"* Jesus asks the second question, because he knows that the answer to the first, why are you weeping, is also the answer to the second, whom do you seek.

This is true even for us today. The answer to our crying, to our pain, to our despair is to seek Jesus Christ. He is the answer to everything that troubles us in our life. We all know too well that whenever we look somewhere else, searching for peace, hope, love apart from Christ, we always find emptiness, disappointment, and even more sadness. Only Jesus Christ is the one who changes crying to hope, who can heal even the most painful wounds, and who changes death to life - and that is precisely why we must seek him at all times.

Mary in today's Gospel sought persistently and the Lord fulfilled her desire even more completely than she could ever imagine. Jesus wants this for us as well. In times when we will be in pain and we will want to hide it and be strong, let us seek Jesus who perfectly fills our hearts with His resurrection joy. Only then will any sadness and pain become moments for us to truly meet Christ.

The road to Emmaus

**Easter Wednesday,
April 23**

Today's readings:
First Reading: Acts 3: 1-10
Responsorial Psalm: Psalms 105: 1-2, 3-4, 6-7, 8-9
Alleluia: Psalms 118: 24
Gospel: Luke 24: 13-35

Today we have before us one of the most beautiful and famous encounters with Christ. It is the encounter of two disciples with the risen Christ. It is a truly wonderful event, which is captured only by Luke's Gospel which makes it all the more special.

The road to Emmaus is a beautiful event, but for us, it is mainly a spiritual event, for it reveals to us the truth about ourselves and about our relationship with Christ. It shows us how Jesus opens our eyes, destroys our spiritual blindness and with his word introduces us to the truth, so that we can fully know him and then bear witness to him.

Looking at this event we notice two very sad disciples, one of them named Cleopas. Church tradition fills in the name of the other as Simon, the son of Cleopas. These two were no ordinary disciples of Jesus, as according to tradition, Cleopas is the brother of Joseph, the foster father of Jesus. Therefore, these two, being related to Jesus, knew very well who Jesus was. It is also worth mentioning that Jesus appears to all his relatives - these two, and according to tradition also to his mother Mary. Going back to Cleopas and Simon, no doubt they spent a lot of time with Jesus, maybe even during his youth when Jesus was growing up in Nazareth. Later, they saw his deeds and his miracles, they listened to his words, they certainly heard Jesus say that he would die and rise from the dead, but today we see that they do not recognize him at all. How could it be that these two did not recognize Jesus, their own family?

We read that their eyes were covered so that they would not recognize him and this is precisely because the Lord had a plan for them. Sometimes it is like this in our lives. The Lord educates us in such a way that he allows us to walk in the dark, for our own benefit, so that we grow in our relationship with Jesus and with our loved ones. We see this here too. These two had their idea about Jesus *"we had hoped that he was the one to redeem Israel,"* and when it did not come true, they gave up. However, just like them, we too are very lucky, because God loves us so much that he will not abandon us even when we become disappointed in him or when we had imagined things differently. Even in those situations, God educates us for himself as he knows what he is doing. In the Gospel, Jesus wanted to correct their idea of him and as we see, they listened to Jesus with burning hearts as he explained everything to them.

In our own lives, we must be careful that our own ideas do not get in the way of Jesus and his plans for us, which are realized even when we do not fully understand. Perhaps our eyes are closed and maybe it does not go the way we would like, but we must never think that we are alone or have been abandoned. But how do we do this? Can we ourselves force our eyes open to see? It is not far fetched to say that we cannot, for that lies only in the power and will of God, however, as we see today, it is God who meets us on our path, even if it is in the opposite direction of what He wants. God is the one who comes into our lives and reveals himself to us in such a way that we are able to see him. He comes to work with us and gives us the graces we need to answer him. This is seen beautifully when the hearts of these two disciples burn with love as Jesus slowly reveals to them everything about him in the Holy Scriptures. All they had to do was to hear what Jesus was saying, to truly be hearers of the Word of God.

And not only through the Word of God, but even more so at table with Christ, in the breaking of the bread of life - there too we come to know Jesus. The closer we get to him and try to know him, the more he reveals himself to us, but it doesn't end there, because as soon as these disciples recognized Christ, they ran to proclaim him to the others. They couldn't contain that joy that burned in their hearts as he completely revealed himself to them. Their encounter with Christ was so very powerful that it moved their hearts and changed their lives.

In this life, we are on the road to Emmaus very often, and our eyes are often covered. But as we heard today, it can be for our benefit. Even when we do not understand, let us not run away, because the Lord will not leave us blind forever, but He will meet us on our way. May we be attentive to his word, may we often break bread with him in the Eucharist, and surely he will appear to us. Let us ask the Lord today, that every encounter with him changes us for the better and let us ask for it fervently, so that he may resurrect our faith and fill us with that same Easter joy these two disciples were filled with.

Peace of Christ

**Easter Thursday,
April 24**

Today's readings:
First Reading: Acts 3: 11-26
Responsorial Psalm: Psalms 8: 2ab and 5, 6-7, 8-9
Alleluia: Psalms 118: 24
Gospel: Luke 24: 35-48

Today we continue from the Gospel we heard yesterday. The apostles announce to the two disciples of Emmaus that the Lord has truly risen from the dead and they also announce to them their joy, that they have recognized him alive in the breaking of bread. To one another they announce the great joy that the resurrection of Christ brings to the heart.

And suddenly, Jesus stands in their midst and says "*peace to you.*" What a powerful moment - just as they were announcing their joy, Christ appears and blesses them. Christ blesses them with the peace that he announces to them before his death. How important is this peace for us today as well - we surely do not want to live without it. The peace of Christ is not worldly peace, but it is inner peace, such as the world and nothing in the world can give. However, we see the apostles are perplexed and still do not understand, reason has not yet caught up with the heart. In that moment, Christ himself must open up their minds to understand everything he was referring to in the Holy Scriptures. Christ helps them understand that every page of Holy Scripture speaks of him, as he alone is their fulfillment. No doubt, this is quite a lot to take in and we will see that it will take the apostles a few more encounters with Jesus to really understand it all. In truth, all uncertainty in their hearts will be dispelled 50 days later at Pentecost - up until then, Jesus will work with them.

We too sometimes do not understand. The heart would like to believe, but sometimes the mind does not understand and therefore we too need to pray for an encounter with Christ, and maybe not just one, but many. Encounters where he may open our minds so that we may better understand his word and live it better. It is a work in progress - no one has ever completed it, as we are to work on it until we meet Christ in heaven. Up until then, we are to accept the Peace of Christ in our lives and then work with Christ just as the apostles did, and so become everyday more authentic witnesses of his resurrection.

On Jesus' word

Easter Friday,
April 25

Today's readings:
First Reading: Acts 4: 1-12
Responsorial Psalm: Psalms 118: 1-2 and 4, 22-24, 25-27a
Alleluia: Psalms 118: 24
Gospel: John 21: 1-14

One of the greatest tragedies for Christians is to return to where they were, that is, to return to that old way of life. We see this in today's Gospel. Peter as the head of the apostles, after meeting Christ, is still not fully convinced. He returns to his work, which he did before he met Christ - he goes fishing. It is a disaster, because it is as if he is throwing away everything he experienced with Christ and the other apostles are doing the same thing.

Of course all is not lost, because in our wanderings, Christ does not leave us alone. He knows that sometimes we will get off the right path and we need him to show us the right path again. That is why he appears to them and makes himself known to them during this miraculous catch of fish. Just as in the beginning of their journey with Christ, when he called them three years ago, when they also miraculously caught fish when they were struggling with it, so too here. Their unsuccessful fishing all night, and then on Jesus' word of casting their net on the other side with an astonishing catch of 153 fish does not go unnoticed. John immediately realizes the similarity of this miraculous catch with their miraculous catch of fish on Jesus' word three years prior on the same spot. At that very moment, John recognizes this stranger as the Lord - as Jesus' word brought them success then, so does it now again. His heart jumps with joy and tells Peter, *"it is the Lord"* who when he hears this immediately jumps into the sea to swim to Jesus.

For us, it is important to know that Christ never gives up on us. No matter how far away we are, where we are with our boat, or even if we do everything backwards, Jesus always tries to reveal Himself to us in such a way that we are able to know Him. He reminds us of key moments in our lives when we recognized Him and on that basis calls us now again to return to Him, even if sometimes it means in a way that is probably not the easiest. We have two examples before us today - John and Peter. John is an example for us to think about events happening to us, and search for Jesus in them, to see him revealing himself to us. Peter is an example for us to act on that realization, no matter what the circumstance, to jump into the water without fear and swim to Jesus. For us today, it is essential for us to be mindful, to have open hearts, and to be attentive to what is going on around us, for it may just be Jesus who is calling us to return to him and experience fullness with Him.

Meet Jesus often

**Easter Saturday,
April 26**

Today's readings:
First Reading: Acts 4: 13-21
Responsorial Psalm: Psalms 118: 1 and 14-15ab, 16-18, 19-21
Alleluia: Psalms 118: 24
Gospel: Mark 16: 9-15

Today's gospel is known as the older and later added longer ending to Mark's Gospel. Some claim that his Gospel originally ended with the verse immediately before, specifically the angels' message to Mary Magdalene that Jesus is not in the tomb, that he has risen from the dead. What is added, is a verse-by-verse summary of what the other Gospels say, which in turn gives Mark's Gospel a more complete conclusion, being today's text. Even the Greek grammar of these last verses doesn't fit with the rest of Mark's gospel, but that doesn't matter, as it is the Word of God and it is a nice concise summary.

Noticing the first sentence from today's Gospel, it simply repeats what just happened in previous verses, how Mary

Magdalene came to the tomb. Then, what follows, are the additions from the other Gospels. Mary Magdalene going to announce the empty tomb to the other disciples is from the Gospel of John. Jesus appearing to two disciples on the road to Emmaus is known from the Gospel of Luke. Jesus then appearing to the eleven, is again from the Gospel of John. And the last sentence, about the missionary command to go and proclaim the Gospel to all people, to all nations, is from the Gospel of Matthew. Quite a nice summary but still only one idea prevails throughout this entire section - the disciples did not want to believe that Jesus had risen from the dead. Clearly, it was such a powerful event that it really took time for them to accept it, as it was really unexpected. What is even more mind-blowing, is that even when they met him after his resurrection, they still needed several meetings to actually believe it. In the end, all doubts vanish only after they receive the Holy Spirit at Pentecost.

Like the disciples of Jesus, we too are to be witnesses of His Resurrection, but sometimes we are like his 11 disciples. We struggle to believe sometimes and just one meeting with Jesus is often not enough. We cannot limit our time with Jesus just to once a week or even less. We too, as the disciples, must constantly come to Jesus, meet with him often, listen to him, and let him do his miracles in our lives. Only then will things change. By often meeting Jesus, we come to know him better, like a true friend and so his ways will become more familiar to us and easier for us. No doubt, this is what we want this Easter season and it is why we spend time with Him. Let our hearts be attentive to the presence of Christ, so that his power may be truly realized in our lives, and then we also go out and be his witnesses.

Touch His wounds

Second Sunday of Easter, Mercy Sunday, April 27

Today's readings:
First Reading: Acts 5: 12-16
Responsorial Psalm: Psalms 118: 2-4, 13-15, 22-24
Second Reading: Revelation 1: 9-11a, 12-13, 17-19
Alleluia: John 20: 29
Gospel: John 20:19-31

There is a legend about Saint Martin, that the devil appeared to him one night in the form of the risen Christ. Saint Martin however was not deceived, he asked *"where are your wounds?"*

What Saint Martin saw, can be compared to today's revelation of Christ to the apostles and especially to Saint Thomas. Many see Saint Thomas as a doubter, as the one who did not believe, whose faith died on the cross with Christ. Even in many nations, if not in all, it is used as a certain form of insult: unbelieving Thomas. Yet no doubt, we must admit that this confession of faith by Saint Thomas is one of the most beautiful, if not truly the most beautiful in the whole Bible about Christ: *"My Lord and my God."* This includes everything: dominion, power, divinity. It is not a confession of an impersonal relationship, but of a very deep and personal relationship, his relationship, as he says "my": *my* Lord and *my* God. Everything is included in this simple but profound confession of faith and love to the living and resurrected Christ.

But what led to this beautiful confession is where we want to meditate today. Saint Thomas wanted to see the wounds of Christ, as for him the only real proof that it was the same Jesus Christ who was crucified, that is, the Jesus whom he himself had seen being crucified, watching it all from afar, were the wounds in his hands and his pierced heart. Wounds are for Saint Thomas the proof - not an empty tomb, not sheets in the tomb, but his wounds. After all, he was not born yesterday, he knows exactly what death is. He knows that his Lord, Jesus Christ, really died - he saw it with his own eyes and no one will convince him that he is alive if he does not see the wounds and the open side. Interestingly enough, even Saint Martin knew very well that he was unable to utter the words *"My Lord and my God"* if he did not first see the wounds of Christ.

And here comes a very powerful moment for Thomas. Jesus acknowledges his request, comes into the locked room and shows him his wounds: *"Put your finger here, and see my hands; and put out your hand, and place it in my side."* Shock! What he wanted becomes a reality, a direct invitation from Christ: *touch my wounds,* touch those wounds that bled out of love for you! What else could Thomas say but fall to the ground in amazement and exclaim with all his heart *"My Lord and my God."* By touching the wounds, Jesus resurrected Thomas' faith: *"do not be faithless, but believing."*

Not by looking at the Risen Christ was Thomas freed from all doubts, but by touching the wounds of Christ. The Risen

Christ showed him that suffering is never forgotten, and that no one's suffering is in vain. Wounds remain wounds. He showed him that wounds are the only place where the seeker and the doubter can truly touch God. Today, Christ identifies himself with all those who suffer, with all those who also have wounds. It only makes sense, if one is to believe in Christ, to be able to exclaim *"My Lord and my God,"* it can only be done if they also touch the wounds of Christ. These wounds are the testimony of our redemption, and where can I find these wounds, if not in the hands of my neighbors. All the painful wounds, all the miseries of the world, all my wounds, their wounds, our wounds, all are also the wounds of Christ, which all together become the place where we encounter God. He is a God that suffered, but was glorified through his wounds.

This is as if Christ wanted to tell Thomas, and at the same time to all of us: *only where you touch human suffering, where you sympathize with the suffering, where you touch wounds - only there will you know that I am alive, that I am God, that I am the Lord. You will meet me wherever people suffer and cry so never hide from them, do not run away from any of these encounters, do not be afraid of them, do not be afraid of the wounds, just believe! Let my wounds be a source of strength for you and a testimony of love, that love that is stronger than death, that it bears all things, believes all things and endures all things.*

Touching the wounds of Christ goes hand in hand with today's feast of Divine Mercy. There is no other path to God than the one that leads through the wounds of Christ and his pierced heart. My God is a wounded God! What a paradox: the source of God's mercy is precisely the wounds of Christ and his pierced heart. Let us touch his holy wounds, let us draw strength there, so that we may be the blessed ones also, and together with Thomas fall to the ground and exclaim: *"My Lord and my God."*

Born anew

Monday 2nd week of Easter, April 28

Today's readings:
First Reading: Acts 4: 23-31
Responsorial Psalm: Psalms 2: 1-3, 4-6, 7-9
Alleluia: Colossians 3: 1
Gospel: John 3: 1-8

Even today, the Lord Jesus is still calling people to His Church. Even though the media tries to discourage us, that the Church is weak, dying and similar delusions, exactly the opposite is true. The Church is growing! Every year, over a hundred thousand people enter the Church. In 2022, 13 million people were baptized and so accepted Christ as their Lord. They recognized that there is life in Him, and today they grow in love living by receiving the sacraments and so become witnesses of God's great love.

In today's Gospel we notice the importance of this fact when the Lord Jesus answers Nicodemus about the necessity of being born anew. *"Unless one is born anew, he cannot see the kingdom of God."* This *"born anew"* is unclear to Nicodemus and maybe even for us. What does it mean? What does it mean for us? Jesus expands on this: *"unless one is born of water and the Spirit, he cannot enter the kingdom of God."* Jesus has in mind not to be born again physically, but spiritually - born of water and the Holy Spirit. The body decays, it is earthly, but what is spiritual remains for eternity. Therefore, the Lord Jesus emphasizes the necessity of being born anew of water and the Holy Spirit! Jesus wants spiritual rebirth through baptism. Jesus wants people to experience with Him the deep spiritual significance of the great Easter mystery - to die to one's old life and rise with Christ to new life! To leave what was, and look up, where Christ is, glorified and resurrected.

But we must also realize that this is not a one-time event. To be born of water and the Holy Spirit, and therefore baptism and confirmation and that is it, done! It must never be so. Once one is born anew, he is to live as a new creation! Every day we should live these sacraments, to nurture and let grow the graces we receive in them. Every day we are to die with Christ and rise with him to new life, and especially in the little things of everyday life, which are often more difficult than the big things. Only after such cooperation with Christ, everyday throughout our lives, will we be able, as Christ says, to enter the Kingdom of God. Let us do this with Nicodemus, let us live our baptismal confession - not only I believe, but also "I actively live".

Serve out of love

Tuesday, Catherine of Siena, Virgin, Doctor, April 29

Today's readings:
First Reading: Acts 4: 32-37
Responsorial Psalm: Psalms 93: 1ab, 1cd-2, 5
Alleluia: John 3: 14-15
Gospel: John 3: 7b-15

They *"were of one heart and soul."* Today's reading from the Acts of the Apostles encourages us to follow the example of the apostles and the early Church - to be generous towards others, to notice others as well as their needs, and to help or serve them accordingly. Only when we do that will we have one heart and one soul. No need to go out and do great big acts, we can easily serve each other in this way in our own household and towards our neighbors.

We hear that Barnabas served what he had - he sold his field and gave it to the community. The Lord probably does not want us to give everything away, as if we don't have anything, it is hard to help others, but he certainly wants us to serve with what we have. We all have our talents and strong qualities -

God gave us them to use, to go and use them to the service of others. In anything I do, I should not sow for only my personal gain, but sow so that others can also benefit from it.

Furthermore, when we love, we serve very willingly, because we do it out of love for that person. Let this be our only criteria - to serve all out of love. This we, we will be like Christ, we will be like the early Church - they also helped each other out of love! As followers of Christ, we are to excel in serving out of love. Let us ask the Lord to give us a willing spirit of service towards everyone.

God's immeasurable love for us

Wednesday 2nd week of Easter, April 30

Today's readings:
First Reading: Acts 5: 17-26
Responsorial Psalm: Psalms 34: 2-3, 4-5, 6-7, 8-9
Alleluia: John 3: 16
Gospel: John 3: 16-21

How great is God's love for us. Listening to the Gospel today invites us to slow down in our life and notice the great love that God has for us ever since creation. In the beginning, God's love was so great, that he created us in His own image. Like the potter molding the clay, he lovingly formed man and as he looked at him, he said that he is very good. All of creation is good in the eyes of God, but man is very good.

However, as time went on, man wandered away from God and sinned. This opens up a new chapter for all of humanity - how to get back to God? How to live again in his presence? For humanity alone it is impossible to achieve this, as we cannot even grasp eternity, let alone reach the heights of God. Without his help, we would still be in darkness and sin. But God never abandons his creation, let alone that creation of which he said is very good. In the fullness of time, God sends his Son to become man.

God the Son becoming man is such a pivotal moment in the history of mankind, as with it everything changes. No more is man far from God, no more is he unable to reach God, for it is God who makes the first step towards mankind and takes upon himself everything that is human and what means to be human. This means, that God loves us so much, that he himself descends to our level to meet us face to face and experience everything that we experience - love, joy, sadness, paid, even death - so that we could forever have him by our side and walk all these experiences with him. Never alone, but with God, who also went through it all as man, as Jesus Christ, and now holds our hand and guides us to get through it like he did - through all tribulations to victory - through the cross to salvation.

There truly is no greater love than this. Simply meditating a few moments about this fact brings one to deep admiration and adoration of God who so dearly loves us. Knowing this and acting on it brings life and light into our days and lives - Jesus brings us this light to dispel the darkness around us. Sure, we will never fully understand this immense and immeasurable love of God for us, because His ways are not our ways and His thinking is not our thinking, but what we can do is give ourselves to him completely and adore him in our hearts with our love at all times. God is waiting for our humble heart that will love him and follow him in the light he sends us. May we always remember his great love for us and so truly do our best to also love him and others in return.

Work to be sanctified

**Thursday, St. Joseph the worker,
May 1**

Today's readings:
First Reading: Acts 5: 27-33
Responsorial Psalm: Psalms 34: 2 and 9, 17-18, 19-20
Alleluia: John 20: 29
Gospel: Matthew 13: 54-58

Today we celebrate the feast of Saint Joseph the Worker. It is a fairly young feast, some may even remember that it was introduced into the calendar in 1955 by Pope Pius XII to oppose the communist Labor Day. The Church rightly chose this date, May 1, to give a deeper spiritual meaning to this feast, to *correctly* explain what work is and what it means for the integrity of man. The Church so attempted to bring the spirit of Christ into this "Labor Day".

From today's Gospel, we see that work and chores are not everything. We hear the people in Nazareth: *"Where did this man get this wisdom and these mighty works? Is this not the carpenter's son?"* These people know Jesus as the carpenter's son, and that's how they have labeled him - he is nothing more for them. But sure enough, Christ has a big surprise for all of them. Work doesn't define us nor determines who we are, but it helps us to be the kind of person God wants us to be. It's not about doing more, but about being more, about being more human. We are to work so that not only my integrity increases, but also that of those around me, so that others are sanctified through my work.

You have certainly had the experience of a good, quality job, where you were treated and served in an exemplary manner, compared to one where you felt bad, or even regretted asking anything at all. Work is supposed to sanctify us, it is supposed to make each of us more human in the full sense of the word, just as the Lord wants us to be.

That is why we celebrate Saint Joseph, the worker, today, because he is an example to us of what work should mean to us. In him we see that we are more than our work, we are more than the economy. In him we see that work should not be an end for us, but a means to becoming better. He was a worker, but it did not hinder him from his other duties, and surely never defined him so that he would falter in helping Mary raise Jesus. He is a shining example for us to be true to our work, and true to ourselves as children of God. May Saint Joseph intercede for us and help us to sanctify ourselves in the work that we do and so also help others grow and be sanctified.

Entrust it to God

Friday, Athanasius, Bishop, Doctor, May 2

Today's readings:
First Reading: Acts 5: 34-42
Responsorial Psalm: Psalms 27: 1, 4, 13-14
Alleluia: Matthew 4: 4b
Gospel: John 6: 1-15

Today, both the first reading and the Gospel have similar ideas and that is: when we are confronted with something difficult, let us entrust it to God's care. It sounds so easy to leave it to the Lord and also believe that he will take care of it, but as we all know very well, this is often quite difficult.

Looking at the readings today, in the first reading, we see the situation in which the apostles were by the authorities absolutely forbidden to speak about Jesus. They want to do what Jesus told them, to evangelize, but are met with restrictions. Similarly in the Gospel, the disciples are faced with the dilemma of feeding the large crowd that followed Jesus, they want to help, but finding so much food is in their eyes impossible and hopeless.

No doubt, both of these situations are difficult for the disciples. If they were to manage them by their own wit and power, they would have failed. Gamaliel reminds everyone that standalone teachings apart from God do not last, but fade away after time, and in the Gospel, feeding so many in a short time with no resources is down right impossible. However, in both situations, the disciples are not alone. In both, they managed to overcome the problem only because of the power of God. They entrusted the whole problem to Christ, and he took perfect care of it. In one case he miraculously fed everyone present and in the second, after getting a punishment they were released and so freely continued to spread the Good News of Jesus Christ.

For us, in our everyday situations or problems, sometimes we trust God very little. But we are today encouraged to entrust everything to God, everything we go through, so that he will take care of it. However, not in a passive way, that we won't do anything and just wait for God's intervention. But to wait actively for the Lord, to be receptive to God's Spirit and his inspirations, to pray and to listen to what he tells us. No doubt, if we put all our worries into God's hands and believe he will take care of it, sooner or.later the solution will appear. Sometimes difficult, but it is what God wants from us - to trust in Him and believe he can do it for us. So let's try to make this a habit, entrusting everything to God. Next time we are faced with anything, let us stop searching on our own, but entrust it entirely to God, pray and wait, and believe that He will take care of it. No doubt He will surprise and amaze us with his solutions and even miracles.

Bring others to Jesus

Saturday, Philip and James, Apostles Feast, May 3

Today's readings:
First Reading: First Corinthians 15: 1-8
Responsorial Psalm: Psalms 19: 2-3, 4-5
Alleluia: John 14: 6b, 9c
Gospel: John 14: 6-14

We celebrate the feast of two apostles, James and Philip. We celebrate them together today because their Holy remains came to Rome together. These two apostles encourage us and help us today in our efforts to follow Christ. Even though we encounter all kinds of things, from Jesus we know that only those who endure to the end will be saved. James and Phillip testified and preached about Christ, they persevered to the end, and today we celebrate them for it. Let us all ask these great men of our faith for perseverance in faith and a firm rooting in Christ.

Unfortunately, we don't know much about James and just a little more about Philip. Philip appears several times in the Gospel, but only in the Gospel of John. The Evangelist refers to him as one of the first disciples of Jesus along with Peter and

Andrew. Jesus called Philip with a simple: *Follow me,* and he got up and followed Jesus. After a short time, he was so convinced that Jesus was the Messiah, so great was his joy that he ran to his friend Nathanael to tell him that he had found the Messiah. Nathanael is a little skeptical at first, at first glance, he is not sure if Jesus is the Messiah. He asks: the one from Nazareth, can anything good come from Nazareth? Philip is the one who encouraged him further, saying *"come and see."* Nathanael then upon meeting Christ, is immediately convinced and also becomes a disciple of Jesus. In another place, some Greeks came to Jerusalem and they asked Philip about Jesus. They wanted to see Jesus and it is again Philip, together with Andrew, that leads them to Christ.

What do we see here and what can we learn? What does Philip actually do? Philip is the one who brought others to Jesus. Philip was absolutely convinced that Jesus was the Messiah, and so he wanted everyone to know him too, he wanted everyone to meet Christ. In addition, he hears from Jesus in another place in the Gospel, that nothing in the world is more important than getting to the Father. So naturally, Phillip wants to see him and asks, *"Lord, show us the Father, and we shall be satisfied."* Jesus answers him beautifully, that He is the image of the Father and whoever follows Him, who *is the way, the truth and the life,* will have communion with the Father, will perform miracles by the power of Christ, will testify to everyone about God's love and will be saved.

What is our task? We are here, reading this book, because Jesus also called us: *"Come, follow me"* and we went. We follow him, because we were and still are convinced that *He is the way, the truth, and the life*. But keeping this for ourselves is not enough, we need to strive for one more thing, we also must do what Philip did - bring others to Christ by our example and way of life.

Let us ask Saint Philip and Saint James today, that we may not be ashamed of our faith, but joyfully testify everywhere and to everyone about Christ, who saved us, redeemed us, and loves us very much. May they intercede for us and help us everyday bring others to Jesus just like they did.

Obedience to Christ

Third Sunday of Easter,
May 4

Today's readings:
First Reading: Acts 5: 27-32, 40b-41
Responsorial Psalm: Psalms 30: 2 and 4, 5-6, 11-12, 13
Second Reading: Revelation 5: 11-14
Gospel: John 21: 1-19

This Gospel is truly beautiful, and maybe one of the most beautiful parts of the entire Bible. The questions that Christ asks Peter are definitely also for us - *do you love me?* Like Peter we too should answer humbly and truthfully. But apart from these questions, today we want to pause for a moment at another part of the Gospel, specifically when the disciples are waiting for Jesus.

We see that the disciples go fishing, but that night they caught nothing. When day had come, Jesus stood on the shore without the disciples knowing it was him. Jesus asks them: *"Children, have you any fish?" They answered him, "No." He said to them, "Cast the net on the right side of the boat, and you will find some."* They cast the net on Jesus' word, and because of the multitude of fish they caught that very moment, they were no longer able to haul it in.

Again, as John likes it, we see another clear contrast here. When the disciples were fishing by themselves, they didn't catch anything and when the Lord asked them if they caught anything, they had to admit that they didn't. This reminds us of Christ's Word: *"He who abides in me, and I in him, he it is that bears much fruit, for apart from me you can do nothing."* Seeing their struggle, Jesus commands them to cast the net from the other side and there they will find fish. Let us notice, Jesus does not say *maybe* there you will find, but Jesus shows certainty and knowledge: *there you will find*. In all honesty, what is the difference between the right side of the boat and the left side? There is no difference, or maybe only that it's just two meters further. But really, what is the difference between the left side of the boat, where the disciples were catching, and the right side, where Christ commanded them? It is obedience to Christ, to the Word of God - they did as the Lord said and it brought them success.

What a simple yet so often difficult thing for us to do: to be obedient to the Word of God. Jesus makes it clear, whoever does as the Lord says, and does not push their own agenda, but obeys the Lord, receives an abundance of God's blessing. Such a person will catch such an amount of God's blessing that they will not be able to fully pull it in.

What a great reflection for today: are we obedient to the word of God? Are we working (fishing) alone without Christ, or together with Christ on his Word? Are we letting ourselves be led by the Spirit of God so that we can gather God's blessings in abundance? No doubt we all want God's blessings in our lives. So let us keep this Gospel in mind and heart. Do everything according to Christ's word and never on our own. And not only that, but also really pay attention to the Word of God, obey God in all things and so truly be able to receive his blessings in abundance.

Why are we searching for Jesus?

Monday 3rd week of Easter,
May 5

Today's readings:
First Reading: Acts 6: 8-15
Responsorial Psalm: Psalms 119: 23-24, 26-27, 29-30
Alleluia: Matthew 4: 4b
Gospel: John 6: 22-29

As we already know and has been shown multiple times, the Gospel of John offers us contrasts, for example, John's common contrast of emptiness and then abundance. The Lord Jesus is the one who fills our emptiness with himself, but he also expects something essential from us - to actually accept what he gives us.

Today, after the miraculous multiplication of the loaves and fishes, Jesus travels by boat to another place. We see that many people are looking for Jesus, but as the Lord himself reveals to us, they are looking for him for the wrong reason: *"you seek me, not because you saw signs, but because you ate your fill of the loaves."* We clearly understand that this is not a good reason, because it is only an earthly reason - just here and now. Here again the contrast of John's Gospel appears: Jesus offers them himself, the bread of eternal life but they seek him for ordinary food, because they are hungry. Jesus offers them an eternal gift - they are looking for an earthly gift.

In the Gospel, this is not the only contrast. The crowd really does not understand what is happening before their eyes, what Christ is actually doing and saying. He tells them about the food that remains for eternal life and they ask him about the power to do the works of God. They are still thinking about being filled and for them this is the most important thing. Seeing that they still do not understand, Christ tries to explain it to them: *this is the work of God, that you believe in him whom he has sent.* So Jesus wants them to believe in Him, to rely on Him, to leave everything to Him, and not try to find fullness outside of Him.

What about us, and how did we understand? It is true that we too sometimes run after those things that are of this earth. We too sometimes emphasize what is not so essential and then we miss out on what is truly important. It is a shame, but just as Jesus does not give up on the crowd when they do not understand so also in our lives, He does not give up on us when we do not understand. On the contrary, He constantly tries to explain it to us, in various ways, through people, events, situations. He constantly calls us to Himself to believe in Him, to receive His body and so have life. We should never take those situations lightly - they too are gifts from God.

May today's prayer from the Gospel: *"Lord, give us this bread always"* - be our prayer too, that we may not seek first this world and earthly gifts, but Jesus Christ, the food that remains for eternal life.

Another sign?

**Tuesday 3rd week of Easter,
May 6**

Today's readings:
First Reading: Acts 7: 51-60
Responsorial Psalm: Psalms 31: 3cd-4, 6 and 7b and 8a, 17 and 21ab
Alleluia: John 6: 35ab
Gospel: John 6: 30-35

Today we continue in the Gospel exactly where we left off yesterday. However, what now follows is quite comical. We saw how the crowd witnessed the miraculous multiplication of the loaves yet now, when Christ tells them to believe in him, they ask him for a sign.

"What sign do you do, that we may see, and believe you? What work do you perform?" It is almost unbelievable that they are asking this of Jesus at his very moment. It is as if they had completely forgotten that he had just performed the miracle of the multiplication of the loaves. However, again, John wants to show by contrast an important truth. We hear that the crowd remembers the manna they received from heaven so long ago

- but they do not remember the multiplication of the loaves, which happened just two days ago. Furthermore, when Jesus tries to explain to them a second time that they are still only looking for what is earthly and here is something better, eternal: true bread from heaven - they demand it: *"Lord, give us this bread always."* It is not yet clear to us whether they understood what such bread is, but the Lord then reveals to them that the eternal food is himself, and whoever wants to live forever must come to him, receive him.

Here we can definitely reflect on how this occurs in our own lives. How often do we demand Jesus for another sign, even though there are already so many around us. How often are we like this crowd, witnessing something amazing with Jesus and then forgetting it soon after? It's like we don't even have time or want to ponder and meditate on what happened, but just want the thrill of another experience. It surely is not about chasing experiences but living each moment with Christ to the fullest. Let us ask Jesus today for the grace to really live each moment of our lives and never just chase sensations.

I am the Bread of Life

Wednesday 3rd week of Easter,
May 7

Today's readings:
First Reading: Acts 8: 1b-8
Responsorial Psalm: Psalms 66: 1-3a, 4-5, 6-7a
Alleluia: John 6: 40
Gospel: John 6: 35-40

For the third day today, we are listening to Jesus' presentation of the Bread of life. In yesterday's Gospel, Jesus was slowly building up to the truly most crucial and climactic moment in this whole dialogue with the crowd. Today that moment is revealed to us when Jesus clearly and openly says: *"I am the bread of life; he who comes to me shall not hunger, and he who believes in me shall never thirst."*

No longer is it unclear - Jesus alone is the bread of life and he is the fulfillment of the manna sent from heaven during the times of Moses. Jesus is the bread of life for all who wish to never hunger again. Of course, not in the sense of food that goes into our stomachs and fills us physically, but in the spiritual sense, Jesus feeds us with himself which has such power in it that it lasts till eternity. But as it always is with whatever Jesus says, it is never just a one way thing - we are required to give our response to him. Our response to the fact that he is the bread of life is whether we believe him or not. *"He who believes in me shall never thirst. But I said to you that you have seen me and yet do not believe."* It is not enough to just say we believe, but we also have to act on this belief. True belief in Christ brings actions, as faith without actions is dead faith or at most is just knowledge of Christ. We know that even the demons know about Christ, but that is not enough to actually live in God's presence. True belief with actions brings true life in Christ.

So how will we respond to Christ? Do we believe in him as he wants it, which means also by our actions? Our belief must be active, must be alive, for this is what Jesus is searching for - active witnesses to his love. May we never fall into laziness with our faith, thinking that the minimum will be enough - it may just happen that it won't be. Let's not risk that. We need to be active, we need to strengthen ourselves on our path following Jesus and that also means partaking in the breaking of the bread of life, which is Jesus in the Eucharist. May we ask today for greater love towards Jesus hidden in the Eucharist and receive him in this sacrament of love more and more often.

Anyone who eats, will live forever

**Thursday 3rd week of Easter,
May 8**

Today's readings:
First Reading: Acts 8: 26-40
Responsorial Psalm: Psalms 66: 8-9, 16-17, 20
Alleluia: John 6: 51
Gospel: John 6: 44-51

In today's Gospel, Christ very strongly emphasizes: *"No one can come to me unless the Father who sent me draws him."* One could say that this could sound quite selective and elitist, but in reality it is not, because the Father does not have favorites, but truly draws everyone to himself. God truly gives everyone enough grace to work with to achieve salvation with his help, the only question is whether they cooperate with that grace or not.

We can also add that those who belong to the Church have even greater joy, as they in community eat *"the bread which comes down from heaven"* and so will *"not perish."* God himself gives himself as food to us, because he wants us to live with him forever. He knows very well that believing in him is one thing, but he also knows that mankind needs to eat. The parallel Jesus gives, is how the Israelites also believed in God when they fled from Egypt, but also received manna from heaven to strengthen them on their way. They ate the bread that God gave them and it brought them into life, into new life, into the promised land. However, this was still only a foreshadowing of what was to come, and that is the bread of eternal life.

Today, our goal in life is not meant to travel to the promised land somewhere abroad like the Israelites. We are in this world to gain eternal life with God in heaven. However, just like the Israelites were strengthened on their journey, we also on our journey to eternal life are strengthened with the bread of life, with the body and blood of Jesus Christ. Jesus is very clear: whoever eats this bread on the way to eternity will live and will not die. As in the times of Moses, when God nourished his people, today Jesus nourishes us to reach the eternal goal.

Let us pray today for greater reverence to the Eucharist, for the zeal to receive Christ in this sacrament often. Let us cooperate with God's grace so that He may strengthen us on our journey to eternity.

Freedom in Christ

**Friday 3rd week of Easter,
May 9**

Today's readings:
First Reading: Acts 9: 1-20
Responsorial Psalm: Psalms 117: 1, 2
Alleluia: John 6: 56
Gospel: John 6: 52-59

The Acts of the Apostles today describes the conversion of Saint Paul. It is the beginning of Paul's way of the cross, the beginning of his journey following Jesus which in the end leads to glory.

What we learn from this reading today is that every person is subject to God's power. God is the one who calls people to work in his harvest, God is the one who can convert even the biggest sinner, God is the one who guides our life, and if we ever go astray, He knows how to deal with us. It is amazing that without violating our freedom, God always brings us exactly where He wants us to be. Some may object to this saying that God is not fair or even that He does not respect our freedom when He calls us like this, but it must be said that freedom is only true freedom when it is in line with God's will. Jesus is also very clear regarding this subject, only *"if the Son makes you free, you will be free indeed."*

Saint Paul was freed only when the Lord Jesus met him on the road and truly set him free. Today, each one of us also needs this freedom in God. Yet often, too many things hinder God's freedom to be realized in us, as we want things our own way and then very quickly we lose sight of what is truly important and lose sight of the one who can truly set us free.

Let us pray today, that we may be truly free in God, but also pray for the conversion of our loved ones. They need our prayers as they will surely help them on their journey in following Christ. May the Lord meet them, draw them to himself, even if in a radical way, but above all, May God fill them and bless them with true freedom.

To whom shall we go?

Saturday 3rd week of Easter,
May 10

Today's readings:
First Reading: Acts 9: 31-42
Responsorial Psalm: Psalms 116: 12-13, 14-15, 16-17
Alleluia: John 6: 63c, 68c
Gospel: John 6: 60-69

Today, after a few days, we are concluding the entire section on the Eucharist in the sixth chapter of the Gospel of John. Jesus explained to us the essence and importance of the Eucharist and today we see the final reaction of the people: *"This is a hard saying; who can listen to it?"* We can notice that they are truly offended by it and did not want to accept it - it was too difficult for them. Jesus directly addresses this: *"Do you take offense at this? Then what if you were to see the Son of man ascending where he was before?"* In other words: *is this a lot for you to accept? Greater things will come, what will you say then?* Jesus also gives an explanation: *"the spirit that gives life, the flesh is of no avail; the words that I have spoken to you are spirit and life. But there are some of you that do not believe."* What does the Lord mean by this?

We know very well that John likes to use contrasts in his Gospel and the main contrast is between those who believe and those who do not believe. We have heard this in the last few weeks, *whoever believes has eternal life,* in contrast to those who do not believe they do not have eternal life. Therefore, in order to receive Jesus' words, which are Spirit and life, faith is needed, the flesh is not enough - it is not enough to just know about these things, to look at the sacraments and the Eucharist superficially, and to live one's life only according to the flesh. This is not enough - let us remember when Christ miraculously multiplied the loaves and fishes - the crowd followed Jesus as this they understood - food, but when Jesus began to speak to them about the Spirit, about faith, about the bread that remains for eternal life and that it must be eaten - then their reaction was *"This is a hard saying."* They looked at everything only with their eyes, only with the flesh - the things of the spirit were far from their hearts.

To truly understand and receive what the Lord is saying, we need to look with our heart, spirit and faith. These three are all given to everyone by God as gifts, so there really is no excuse. Even today, each one of us has received these gifts, therefore let us not throw away what the Lord has given us. Many threw it all away as we hear: *"After this many of his disciples drew back and no longer went about with him."* Many even today, carelessly throw away these great gifts from God and it is truly sad as even the Lord is sad about it: *"Will you also go away?"* You also do not have faith? Do you not want life?

At this moment, we see the most beautiful contrast of Jesus' whole speech: the strongest contrast to those who do not believe. Peter answers for all of us *"Lord, to whom shall we go? You have the words of eternal life."* Peter answers for all who want to believe, who want to listen to Christ, who have come to know that only Christ gives life and that truly nothing else in the world is equal to Christ. May Peter's answer of loyalty and devotion to Christ also be our answer in every situation, when it is difficult and when we do not understand: *"Lord, to whom shall we go? You have the words of eternal life, and we have believed, and have come to know, that you are the Holy One of God."*

I am the Good Shepherd

Fourth Sunday of Easter,
May 11

Today's readings:
First Reading: Acts 13: 14, 43-52
Responsorial Psalm: Psalms 100: 1-2, 3, 5
Second Reading: Revelation 7: 9, 14b-17
Alleluia: John 10: 14
Gospel: John 10: 27-30

Jesus' words today describe a situation as old as humanity itself. Since Adam and Eve nothing has truly changed and we encounter it every day, namely, humanity is like a flock of sheep. This of course is not meant negatively, but in the best and most positive sense of the word.

First of all, humanity truly needs a shepherd, a good shepherd, who would truly guard, guide and protect. Secondly, humanity is attacked from every side, it is constantly exposed to danger and since each of us is a human being, each of us is therefore also a sheep and we belong to a flock. The question is, to which flock do we belong, and whose voice do we listen to?

If we very quickly notice the entire history of salvation, we see that there are constantly those who come to man who knock on the door of the sheepfold. They want to enter and want to get into our hearts, into our minds. They want us to trust them, they want us to follow them. It must be made very clear that these are pseudo-shepherds, they pretend to be shepherds who present themselves as great, caring and good, they offer all sorts of things and call: obey me, come after me. It seems that they want us well but in reality it is not true at all. It is clear that this includes various ideologies, opinions, groups that look good on the outside, but in essence are not.

What is the problem here? What does Jesus say? *"He who does not enter the sheepfold by the door but climbs in by another way, that man is a thief and a robber."* We see that *"the thief comes only to steal, kill and destroy."* The various voices that constantly call out to us are those who do not enter the sheepfold by the gate but climb into the sheepfold by some other way. All of these are thieves and robbers, do not care about the sheep and do not know the sheep by name. They attempt to attract from the outside, entice, sometimes even break in by force, sometimes they cunningly disguise themselves as shepherds, just to snatch as many sheep as possible. However these pseudo-shepherds do not know where the good pastures are, the pastures of eternal life, they will never be able to feed the sheep properly and it always ends in hunger, even spiritual death. The Lord Jesus is very clear: *"the thief comes only to steal, kill and destroy."*

In contrast to all these pseudo-shepherds, Jesus presents his role to us: *I am the good shepherd. I am the shepherd of the sheep and the sheep listen to my voice. I call my sheep by name, I walk before them and they follow me because they know my voice, and I lead them out to good pasture.* Only Jesus cares about the sheep, only Jesus knows the sheep by name, only he gives them the pasture of eternal life, and those who follow him do not walk in darkness but walk towards salvation because only Jesus is the way, the truth and the life.

Here we can return to the question: whose voice are we listening to? Is it the voice of Jesus? Is it his word, or do we let ourselves be carried away very quickly by pseudo-shepherds? Every day, we must try to listen to the voice of Jesus and only his voice and not those voices of all those around us, who truly do not wish us well. Only Jesus Christ, the Good Shepherd, leads us to good pastures, where he will give us freedom and fill us with true joy because that is why he came. Jesus himself says: *"I came that they may have life, and have it abundantly."* Let us strive to follow Jesus, let us only listen to his voice and he will bless us so abundantly that we will be truly amazed.

Pray the Psalms

**Monday 4th week of Easter,
May 12**

Today's readings:
First Reading: Acts 11: 1-18
Responsorial Psalm: Psalms 42: 2-3; 43: 3-4
Alleluia: John 10: 14
Gospel: John 10: 1-10

Not very often is a lot of attention given to the Psalms. We hear or even sing them quite often, but rarely do we see any explanation or application to our own lives, which is a real shame, because they are so beautiful, simple and powerful prayers. They include all aspects of life, so easily we can say, if anyone has a problem with prayer, let them start by reading/praying the Psalms. If "I don't know how to pray" describes us today, let us pray the Psalms. Let's open the Psalm book, pick just one, any one of them, and reflect and meditate on it for a day, or for a week and live from what it means to us personally. There is great power in discovering the power of God's Word in one's life.

Today we prayed Psalm 42 and 43 which describe the spiritual dimension of a person's life, or in other words, the ideal. Liturgically it is divided into three parts, so we too will look at it more closely accordingly.

The first part: *"so longs my soul for thee, O God. My soul thirsts for God, for the living God."* Man longs for God, because that is how he is created. Anyone, in order to be happy, needs to first of all fulfill this relationship with God. Anyone who in their life fills this thirst for God first, everything else will fall into place. If a man longs for God and so goes after what is right, he will be happy and so will his wife be happy, because in that case, everything a man does springs from his longing for God. However, he who does not live like this, who does not fulfill this longing for God, will hardly find happiness.

The second part: a person who longs for God prays, calls on God, asks God for his blessings. He asks in prayer: *"send out thy light and thy truth; let them lead me, let them bring me to thy holy hill and to thy dwelling!"* A person who longs for God wants to be led by God, and when God sees this, He brings that person to Himself, into His presence. In the psalm it is represented by the holy hill - a place of meeting with God, a place close to God.

And the third part: a person, finally, when he longs for God and prays, experiences joy and exults over God's blessing in his life. Such a person looks at his life with the eyes of faith, with God's eyes and sees God's hand in everything. Such a person is thankful to God for the good and humbly accepts the bad. He comes to God's altar and gives himself completely to God and keeps nothing for himself. He gives his whole life to God, his heart, soul, problems, joys - he gives everything to God, because he already knows from experience that only God is the only source of his happiness and joy.

So simple and so beautiful. The psalms are so rich with such beauty, we really ought to read/pray them more often. The psalms really have so much to offer us, because they were created by the biblical writer reflecting on his own life with God. This is key, because many of them are attributed to King David who definitely went through a lot in his life, both good and bad, and so that's why there is something in them from every aspect of human life. Let us often enrich our spiritual lives with the beauty of the psalms, let us pray the psalms often, even find our favorite one and apply it to our own lives. There is great power in these psalms, God's power and blessings, may that power truly manifest itself in our lives as we slowly dive into this great spiritual treasure.

Our actions testify about us

Tuesday, Our Lady of Fatima, May 13

Today's readings:
First Reading: Acts 11: 19-26
Responsorial Psalm: Psalms 87: 1b-3, 4-5, 6-7
Alleluia: John 10: 27
Gospel: John 10: 22-30

How many times in life were we surprised to learn that people are not always as they say they are? How do we find out what a person really is like? Is asking them an objective picture of what they really are like? Or even, what do we say about ourselves - how are we? No doubt, it happens that we embellish the good in our lives and take away from the bad. We want to look good in the eyes of others and no doubt it's normal. No one puts their bad qualities in the foreground when they want to be friends with someone. Sure enough, that comes later over time, as they get to know each other in a relationship. However, a lot of what a person is like is shown by the way they behave in individual situations.

Saint John Bosco, knew very well that sports and competitiveness often display the true face of a person. In such situations, even though nothing may be at stake, and one begins to lose, they begin to show their true self - do they accept loss with dignity, or does all morality go out the door just so that they could say they won.

We know very well that good and bad thoughts flow from the heart and subsequently are expressed in actions. If someone presents themselves as kind and attentive, but their actions show otherwise, we very quickly form a more complete opinion about them. Their words may say one thing, but their actions show the truth about them and if it is not pleasant, then more often than not, we tend to avoid such a person.

In today's Gospel we hear the Jews demanding an answer from Christ: *"How long will you keep us in suspense? If you are the Christ, tell us plainly."* No doubt, they certainly expected an answer like: *yes, I am the Messiah*, but they did not receive anything of the sort. Christ answers them a bit differently: *"I told you, and you do not believe. The works that I do in my Father's name, they bear witness to me; but you do not believe."* Honestly, what more did the Jews want? The works of Christ clearly indicate who he is: power over sin, power over disease, power over nature, power over death - whoever really sees all of this and connects all the dots, comes to the conclusion that his testimony is from God and is true.

Today, the same applies to us: sweet and kind words are one thing, but let them be followed by good deeds. No doubt, good deeds are important as John writes in his letter, that as followers of Christ, we should be known by love and by how we love one another. Truly, what is the point of anything, if there is no love? In the words of Paul to the Corinthians: *without love I am like a noisy gong or a clanging cymbal, without love, I am nothing.*

Let us not allow this to be our case. Let not only our words be good, but also our deeds - so that we like this may be like Christ - doing the works of the Father. This way, our example will shine everywhere we go and so give living testimony to all that we truly belong to Christ.

God qualifies the called

Wednesday, Matthias, Apostle Feast, May 14

Today's readings:
First Reading: Acts 1: 15-17, 20-26
Responsorial Psalm: Psalms 113: 1-2, 3-4, 5-6, 7-8
Alleluia: John 15: 16
Gospel: John 15: 9-17

Today we celebrate the feast of Saint Matthias the Apostle. He is the apostle of Jesus Christ who - as we heard in the first reading - was not among the twelve, but was chosen. He was chosen from among those who walked with Christ from his baptism until the ascension, to be a witness to the resurrection of Jesus.

Saint Peter explains to us that it was prophesied – the scripture had to be fulfilled – that one would betray Christ and another would take his place. The truth of the matter is, any one of the twelve could have been the traitor. Each one of them was close to Jesus, they listened to his words, they saw his miracles, but how it played out was up to them – if they cooperated with God's Word and love was their choice. For instance, Peter stumbled – he denied Christ three times, but repented, cooperated with God's love and today he shines with holiness. Judas also stumbled, but he did not repent, he did not want to cooperate with God's love, as he wanted it his way and so he took his own life – with his decision the scripture was fulfilled.

What does all this imply? God does not call the qualified ones, but God qualifies the ones he calls. Peter was not perfect and definitely not qualified, but he let himself be perfected by Jesus. Judas however took everything into his own hands, and it did not end well.

Saint Matthias, like Peter and the other apostles, cooperated with God's grace and let himself be perfected and qualified by Jesus. He is called by God, but that is not the end yet, he still had to show his love for God, that he really meant it, and he truly did so, with his life. Even though we do not know much about him, we know that he was a zealous proclaimer of the Word of God and died a martyr's death for Christ.

Similarly, we are called to follow Christ, like Saint Matthias, but it has not yet been shown what this calling will bring in our lives. So much depends on us, how we will cooperate with God's grace, whether we will let God perfect and qualify us or not. In this regard, doing just the minimum or just what is required, is definitely not enough - we see this in the life of Judas. We must be better and do more, we must let God's Word work in us, so that we really bear fruit, because only in this way, as Christ himself says, will we glorify God.

Let us ask Saint Matthias for the courage and strength to follow Christ, and that he may help us to listen attentively to God's Word with an open heart so that we, like him, may let God perfect us and so bear good fruit and be living witnesses of Jesus Christ.

Persecuted? You are blessed!

**Thursday 4th week of Easter,
May 15**

Today's readings:
First Reading: Acts 13: 13-25
Responsorial Psalm: Psalms 89: 2-3, 21-22, 25 and 27
Alleluia: Revelation 1: 5ab
Gospel: John 13: 16-20

Today, the Gospel passage is quite powerful. Christ explains to us what we can expect if we follow him: *"A servant is not greater than his master."* If we want to belong to Christ, we must realize that everything he went through and as He suffered truly awaits us too. Whether it is persecution, hatred by the world, condemnation or contempt from others, if we want to belong to him, all of this may encounter us. Why? This is because as Jesus says, a servant is not greater than his master, and if they already persecuted the master, they will also persecute his servants.

But the best part is when Jesus says: *"If you know these things, blessed are you if you do them."* Amazing! When we realize that we will be persecuted and know that this is how it works, then we are blessed. The persecution from the world gives us the opportunity to be blessed! Even looking at the world today - so many martyrs have shed their blood for Jesus Christ - they are blessed! But not only martyrs, similarly, we can experience such persecution directly in our family, and from loved ones. We can experience such persecution at work or when we stand for what we believe is right. Many situations in our lives can bring such persecution, but only when we understand it as suffering with Christ and for Christ, we are blessed. Only when we accept this truth do we actually walk with Christ, faithfully after him, joining him on the way of the cross - not to death - but to salvation and glory.

What follows in the Gospel completes the whole picture: *"I am not speaking of you all; I know whom I have chosen; it is that the scripture may be fulfilled, 'He who ate my bread has lifted his heel against me.'"* Here, Jesus is talking about Judas, who did not want to suffer with him, but wanted to go his own way, find his own solution and salvation. Jesus Christ is very clear: such a person cannot be blessed, because he thinks that his plan, his solution and his will is better than God's will and divine plan. Unfortunately, with such behavior, Judas loses Christ as Lord in his life and as we know, ends tragically.

Nothing has changed since then. Jesus' words of warning apply also to us when we want to go our own ways, decide about our lives apart from God, decide that we do not want that persecution or the way of the cross. However, only by the cross is our salvation won. We must realize this if we want to follow Jesus - he gave us the prime example - salvation only comes through the cross! Let us not run from the cross - persecution in our lives brings about that we are blessed. Let us walk the path that the Lord Jesus paved for us and let us accept whatever persecution comes our way knowing that with it, we are walking side by side with Jesus to glory.

Do not worry! Believe!

**Friday 4th week of Easter,
May 16**

Today's readings:
First Reading: Acts 13: 26-33
Responsorial Psalm: Psalms 2: 6-7, 8-9, 10-11ab
Alleluia: John 14: 6
Gospel: John 14: 1-6

All of us have enough of our worries in life, we are not sure how this and that will turn out, we have certain obstacles to overcome and when it all piles up together, it is often very overwhelming and takes away our peace. We as human beings worry and more often than not, does not do us any good.

In today's Gospel, Christ addresses this issue: Let not your heart be troubled! You believe in God, believe also in me. How soothing are these words! Jesus does not want us to be afraid, to be nervous, to worry, in the sense that we worry about what will happen today, tomorrow, the day after tomorrow. Certainly, what is in our power to do, we must do, but the rest must be left to the Lord and his providence. We cannot take it all into our own hearts and minds and worry what will be. We cannot go through life fearful, nervous, sad or even unhappy. If we do experience this, it is probably a sign that we want to have everything under control, in our own hands, and when it does not work out, we are disappointed and sad. That only makes us worry even more and so we spiral down that rabbit hole, once too deep, very difficult to get out. That is no doubt not the right path at all, and if it is our situation, we need to change it fast.

Today, we can start by not looking at things so negatively and evaluating everything according to whether we can do it or not. Christ wants to give us peace of heart, and therefore, we must first and foremost believe in God, in Jesus Christ, and trust him that he can do wonders for us! He doesn't want our hearts to be troubled by this or that - we must first believe in him and he will take care of it. It is definitely human to worry and be concerned about things, but it is divine to believe and trust in God with all our heart, that he will provide. Let us try to do everything in our lives with this in mind - as Saint Augustine put it - *Do what you can, and pray for what you cannot, and so God will grant you the ability to do it.*

Great deeds

Saturday 4th week of Easter, May 17

Today's readings:
First Reading: Acts 13: 44-52
Responsorial Psalm: Psalms 98: 1, 2-3ab, 3cd-4
Alleluia: John 8: 31b-32
Gospel: John 14: 7-14

Today we hear quite an interesting request. Philip wants to see the Father: *"Lord, show us the Father, and we shall be satisfied."* We don't really know what he was expecting, maybe some sensational revelation, something like the revelation of God on Mount Sinai, but Jesus cools him down very quickly when he tells him: *"He who has seen me has seen the Father."*

What does Christ mean? Jesus Christ is the image of the invisible God the Father. When we look at Christ, based on his words and deeds, we come to understand what God the Father is really like. We know that Jesus Christ and the Father are one, therefore, when Christ loves us here on earth, our heavenly Father loves us also - when Christ forgives us, God the Father also forgives us.

Jesus Christ is also, as we know, the Word of God. He is the very Word that comes from the mouth of God, the Word that lifts us up to the Father. When we listen to Christ, we actually listen to the Father, become his children, and gain the ability to do God's great deeds. But what are those deeds? We can summarize them into one - wherever the Gospel values are truly lived, those great deeds are done, and these can truly be any deeds, even small ones - but if they are done with great love - then Christ's words are truly realized even today.

Christ encourages us to do these works, to join him in working the deeds of the Father, and doing even greater deeds than he did. Let us believe these words, let them be words of certainty for us that Christ is with us in everything that we will do and truly believe him when he says: *"Whatever you ask in my name, I will do it."* Let us therefore ask Jesus in our prayers, without fear, and truly believe that he will fulfill it and so help us do God's wondrous deeds.

Missionary of Love

**Fifth Sunday of Easter,
May 18**

Today's readings:
First Reading: Acts 14: 21-27
Responsorial Psalm: Psalms 145: 8-9, 10-11, 12-13
Second Reading: Revelation 21: 1-5a
Alleluia: John 13: 34
Gospel: John 13: 31-33a, 34-35

Probably everyone knows who Saint Mother Teresa is. She worked in the poorest parts of Calcutta in India and many have written about her life and her testimony of love and no doubt her example is very encouraging for our faith, especially when we think that the whole world is collapsing around us - or when we perceive that our own life is collapsing. It is good to encourage ourselves by the examples of the saints, and even by her life and discover the treasure that she had - the source of her strength.

So what was her source, what was the driving force in her? One author in a book about her describes it beautifully when he writes about one of her meetings with a passing gentleman.

It was a morning when, as usual, Mother Teresa was helping the poorest who were lying in the street. She was treating a gentleman who was lying half-dead - cleaning and bandaging his wounds, and as a gentleman who was just passing by saw it - he said to her: *I wouldn't do this even for millions in cash.* Mother Teresa looked at him and replied: *neither would I.*

A short answer, but a very powerful testimony, because by it she showed what was in her - what was in her heart and what was her driving force. With this answer, we also realize that she did not do it for a reward - she did not do it for money and she did not do it for world recognition either, even though she received the Nobel Peace Prize. All of that was unimportant to her as what drove her to do good, to serve the poor, to sacrifice herself for those who could not return the favor was pure love. She did it out of love for God and for her neighbor.

Through her life, we see beautifully that she took to heart the Lord's commandment *"to love one another, even as I have loved you… by this all men will know that you are my disciples."* We become disciples of Christ because of our love. Love alone is the identifying mark of personal closeness to Jesus and without a doubt, Mother Teresa was very close to Christ, she was his disciple because she loved so much. It is truly moving and motivating to see how much good one person - connected to Christ - can do. She did not examine the advantages or disadvantages, but served selflessly, loved to the extreme, loved like Christ.

How do we live this commandment of Christ? How do we love our neighbors? Is it possible to recognize in us that we are disciples of Christ based on our love? At the end of the day, people will not remember what we said or what we did, but how they felt around us. Today, we can change this to whether they felt loved around us. May love be our characteristic, as we too become missionaries of love.

Jesus dwells in us

Monday 5th week of Easter,
May 19

Today's readings:
First Reading: Acts 14: 5-18
Responsorial Psalm: Psalms 115: 1-2, 3-4, 15-16
Alleluia: John 14: 26
Gospel: John 14: 21-26

Each of us has our home, a place where we live - it is our sacred place, where we spend a large part of our lives - ideally, it should be a place where we experience love, joy, peace and happiness. It is a place where we grow up and are formed into the people we are. At home we learn respect and esteem for parents, siblings and towards other people. It is the place where we also encounter problems and work together to solve them constructively. Our home is a place where we should always like to return, because there we feel good and are loved.

But sometimes it happens that big problems arise and our home ceases to be a place of love, joy and happiness. It becomes a place of unrest and quarrels, we slowly start to avoid home and we don't like being there. Why is it so? The answer is found today in the Gospel.

The Lord Jesus says: *"If a man loves me, he will keep my word, and my Father will love him, and we will come to him and make our home with him."* The Lord Jesus makes it clear to us today that He wants to dwell in us, our hearts are to be Jesus' home. Just as Jesus dwells in the love of the Father and the Holy Spirit - and it is a perfect relationship of love - He also wants to dwell in us, to be loved by us. How do we accomplish this and what are the conditions for Christ to dwell in us? Jesus answers: *"If a man loves me, he will keep my word."* This means to live according to the Gospel and to live sacramentally, only then does Christ dwell in us and sanctify us, transforming us into better people.

How true is this also of our homes and in our families. If we love Christ, listen to and keep his Word and live sacramentally - and everyone else in our family also - then our home truly becomes a sacred place where the Lord Jesus himself dwells. In such a home Jesus is truly present, He pours out of his heart His peace, joy and love and the atmosphere in this family is truly blessed. Of course, we know very well that sometimes it is quite difficult to keep his word and we struggle with it, therefore, in order to manage it, we must ask for more love. It actually all really depends on our love, and we all know we can always love more than we already do.

So what do our families look like and what kind of atmosphere reigns in them? Does the Lord Jesus dwell in our families? Does the Lord Jesus dwell in us? Let all our answers be "yes" and let us show Christ that we truly love him by keeping his word and living sacramentally - so that in this way we may always be his beautiful dwellings.

Life in Christ's peace

Tuesday 5th week of Easter
May 20

Today's readings:
First Reading: Acts 14: 19-28
Responsorial Psalm: Psalms 145: 10-11, 12-13ab, 21
Alleluia: Luke 24: 46, 26
Gospel: John 14: 27-31a

Where do we go to find peace? Some may say peace can be found by relaxing in nature, others may say in quiet time with a coffee, and still others with a loved one. The answers may be many. But we know that those moments do not last forever, so where should we go to find true peace? Maybe we are experiencing peaceful days, is this the kind of peace that the Lord Jesus gives us today? Jesus tells us today: *"my peace I give to you; not as the world gives."* If Jesus does not give as the world gives, then what kind of peace does the world give and what kind does Jesus give?

We could say that the world tries to give us peace in all sorts of ways: local security, plans, maybe even world peace, a conflict-free or war-free state, which truly are all good things, but if it is separated from Christ, then it will be very difficult to sustain. We cannot put all our hope into this kind of peace, because it may be here today, but tomorrow might bring a different outcome. We need peace that lasts.

Saint Paul in his letter to the Galatians lists 12 fruits of the Holy Spirit, and one of them is peace. True peace is not something that this material world can give us. We experience true peace within our hearts, true peace is only God's peace which stems from life with him. We can have even the whole world at our fingertips and all the money in the world, and yet, without God, we would never have true peace. We only need to look at any famous singer or actor who lives apart from God - does it look like they have true peace along with all the material things they have? It wouldn't be far fetched to say that they lack true peace.

Only life with Christ is a life in peace. Even if we often go through difficult things and events, if we believe that the Lord will lead us through it, no doubt after a short trial, He will grant us the peace we long for, and if not in this world, then He will certainly give His faithful His eternal peace in His kingdom. Let's strive for this peace of Christ.

Connected to Christ

Wednesday 5th week of Easter,
May 21

Today's readings:
First Reading: Acts 15: 1-6
Responsorial Psalm: Psalms 122: 1-2, 3-4ab, 4cd-5
Alleluia: John 15: 4a, 5b
Gospel: John 15: 1-8

As people, we are in our nature productive. Almost everywhere productivity has become the standard of our life, work and success. It is as if coded into our lives, into our relationships, into the economic system, basically everywhere, and those who are more productive are more rewarded and those who are not or do not offer anything to society, are not interesting or attractive. This can be good but can also be very dangerous, even diabolical if lives must end just because they are not productive for society.

Humanity in general is convinced that productivity is the goal and has become the only possibility of survival. This idea, in connection with today's Gospel, Jesus tells us: *"Every branch of mine that bears no fruit, he takes away, and every branch that does bear fruit he prunes, that it may bear more fruit."* We understand that even for God it is necessary for us to bear fruit in life, so that we are not thrown into the fire. However, this is only part of the whole picture. The priority is not to bear fruit, but to first be connected to Christ, united with him. Before anything else, God wants us to listen to his word and keep it. This means to Jesus Christ and have a deep relationship with him.

Fruit in life – or the absence of it – is a direct consequence of what my love relationship with Christ looks like. Abundance or absence reveals whether we are connected to Christ or not, whether He is the priority for us or rather just productivity. Those who love Christ, bear fruit but those who do not love Christ, who do not want Him in life and do not seek Him, in truth don't even need God the Father to cut them off, because they cut themselves off/ They decide for a life outside of Christ and outside of life, it may no doubt bring productivity - but that is far from Christ, far from love.

This becomes a serious problem - productivity is demanded of us, but true love, service and sacrifice are missing. They are missing because that connection to Christ who is the source of good quality and healthy fruit, which would really move society forward is cut off. Productivity becomes the norm and in such a system, where there is no mercy and no love, terrible things may happen - and in fact do happen.

If our society does not change by all of us starting with that change, with our love, with our faith, with being connected to Christ and giving a good example – who else will stand there and fight for those who are defenseless? Everything stands on our connection to Christ, our love for him and from there, love for others. Christ reminds us today: *"I am the vine, you are the branches... If you abide in me, and my words abide in you, ask whatever you will, and it shall be done for you. By this my Father is glorified, that you bear much fruit, and so prove to be my disciples."* Do we remain in him and in his love? It is truly a relationship of love, and where there is love, there is service, there is sacrifice, there is an abundance of good fruit. May this motivate us to love more, to love Christ, to be connected to him, so that we bear much fruit, because only then will we truly lift our society to higher places and thereby glorify God the Father.

Why do we love?

Thursday 5th week of Easter,
May 22

Today's readings:
First Reading: Acts 15: 7-21
Responsorial Psalm: Psalms 96: 1-2a, 2b-3, 10
Alleluia: John 10: 27
Gospel: John 15: 9-11

Why do we love? Why do we even love anyone? How is it that we love this person more than that person? What is it that creates this love in us? In the first place, it is God himself, as he is Love and out of his love he created us in his image, so etched into our being is the fact that we can love as God loves. But even more than that, since love is a dynamic power, it is not enough that it is part of our being - it must be acted on.

What does this mean? We love because we are loved, because we have met others that love us and through their love, we have learned to love also. Love therefore becomes so powerful because man is so created, that he is moved when he sees that someone loves him, and soon he also loves the one who first loved him. This is how the love of God arises in the heart of man. From love known and experienced, love arises. How important it is to love! What joy it brings to follow in the work of our God, who first loved us even when we were sinners and still loves us today! Jesus makes this very clear in the Gospel: *"As the Father has loved me, so have I loved you; abide in my love."*

To love means to partake in the dynamic love that is constantly flowing from God the Father to the Son, through the Holy Spirit. This brings such power and blessings to our lives, for when we love, we are fully living as God intended us to live. When we love, we truly live up to the image of God in which we are created.

May we never give up on love. May we love, not because others love us, but because God loves us and we have experienced it tremendously in our lives. May we be beacons of love for everyone to see, so that through us, who abide in God's love, may also experience that amazing love that God gives.

I have chosen you

Friday 5th week of Easter,
May 23

Today's readings:
First Reading: Acts 15: 22-31
Responsorial Psalm: Psalms 57: 8-9, 10 and 12
Alleluia: John 15: 15b
Gospel: John 15: 12-17

After going through quite a lot in his life, Saint Augustine famously says: "Love God, and do whatever you please." What a powerful and true statement! It is true, because when we truly love God, everything we do in our life, is done out of love for God. Such a person grows in love each and every day and can truly say that he is friends with God.

No doubt Saint Augustine formed a lot of his theology out of John's Gospel, which so often brings about the theme of love. Even in today's Gospel, Jesus reminds us of the importance of true love. He clearly explains to us what true love looks like - it is sacrifice. To lay one's life for a friend is true love, as it follows the example that Jesus himself gave us - he gave his life for us so that we too may have life.

In addition to that, Jesus gives us two other options in how to experience love - to experience love either as a servant or as a friend. Either we love because we have to, or we love willingly and wholeheartedly. In our lives, at any given moment, one of these two options is dominant. Either we love as servants: we do only the minimum, without love, without interest, all done just because we have to - this neither has value nor changes us for the better. Or, we love as friends, who want to be with Jesus, who want to know him, who want to communicate with him, who want to share this love with others - all out of love for Jesus.

Which of these two is dominant in our life? Are we more like servants or friends? Christ emphasizes: *"I have called you friends... You did not choose me, but I chose you."* Jesus invites us to friendship with him, to a deep relationship of love as He Himself personally chose us - how powerful this is when we truly realize it - we are not some being in the universe just random and by chance, but we are chosen and called by Jesus, by name, to share in his love. What a tragedy if we reject it, if we choose a life without Him, or even the life of a servant.

Today's Gospel invites us to reflect on our love for Jesus. If love for Jesus is in the right place in our lives and hearts and we strive for it, so too will our love for others be in the right place and we will love fully in our relationships. The Lord says: *"You are my friends if you do what I command you."* Let us learn from Christ, let us do what He commands us, let us love Him and our neighbors and sure enough, along the path of our life, we will marvel at His great love for us and abundant blessings given.

The world will hate you!

Saturday 5th week of Easter, May 24

Today's readings:
First Reading: Acts 16: 1-10
Responsorial Psalm: Psalms 100: 2, 3, 5
Alleluia: Colossians 3: 1
Gospel: John 15: 18-21

As humans, we like to be liked by others. We strive to have a good image and try to be amicable wherever we are. We could say it is very normal and it is attractive. We also don't like it when we are not liked by others, as it can be bothersome and so we often try to work on that, to get rid of being on someone's disliked side and so bring harmony back to our lives.

Jesus however paints a very different picture for us today in the Gospel. "If the world hates you, know that it has hated me before it hated you." Jesus reminds us that if we wish to belong to him, we must count on it that we will be met with hatred and persecution. On the one hand, this can be comforting to know, especially when we realize in difficult times, that the hatred from the world confirms to us that we are on the right path, on the path of life. If we were to be loved by the world, we should as Christians worry, because Christ says of those that they belong to the world. We can say it is all a question of who do we want to belong to? We can examine our own lives and see, what is dominant, is it love from the world, or hatred? Friendship with the world means enmity with God. We cannot have both, we must choose.

No doubt this can be a difficult choice for many, and in fact how many have truly fallen away from Christ because they loved the world more than him. This is definitely not a matter to be just left as it is, but we must honestly ask our hearts - who is my master? Who do I love more? Is it the world, or is it Jesus?

"Time has grown very short" as Saint Paul says to the Corinthians. We cannot risk leaving the answer to this for later - the time to answer is now, but truly thinking about it we realize that we already have answered this question, and that is by our lives. The way we live today is exactly our answer, if we love the world more or Jesus more. Whatever it may be today, we have an opportunity to change it right now. Let us ask Jesus for the strength to not be afraid of hatred and persecution from the world, as there we will find the path to glory, just as he did. Through the cross to salvation.

Holy Spirit active in us

**Sixth Sunday of Easter,
May 25**

Today's readings:
First Reading: Acts 15: 1-2, 22-29
Responsorial Psalm: Psalms 67: 2-3, 5, 6 and 8
Second Reading: Revelation 21: 10-14, 22-23
Alleluia: John 14: 23
Gospel: John 14: 23-29

It is not uncommon to hear criticism regarding Christians, that they only pray, sing and follow Christ in Church, but once they go out the door, their deeds testify to something else. On the one hand, we all must beat our chests in repentance and admit that we are sinners, each and every one of us, and we all have something to work on, something to improve. But on the other hand, no matter what we are and who we are, the Holy Spirit works in us, calls us into communion with God, sanctifies our actions, our thoughts, our words, and constantly brings us back into God's presence. This active power working in us is the grace of God, the Holy Spirit working in us, and once we realize it, it becomes clear to us that everything is grace, everything in our lives has the Holy Spirit written on it.

This Holy Spirit, as we hear today, is the Spirit of Jesus Christ - *"the Father will send in my name"*, and as the Spirit of Christ, He goes where He wills. No doubt this is seen in the world, as going where he wills, the Holy Spirit is always active, in every culture, in every religion, in every person, in various degrees and forms. The Holy Spirit works with each and every person, therefore, to criticize Christians because they fall short of perfectly working with the Holy Spirit is very harsh. Not one person perfectly works with the Holy Spirit, as sometimes we don't understand, or what is asked of us is in our view too difficult, or sometimes we even don't want to work with the Holy Spirit when we don't want to pray, don't want to go to church, don't want to go love others. However, even when we go astray like this, deep in our being, the Holy Spirit acts, and calls us out of that darkness to enter the light and encourages us to try to live our faith as best we can.

Will we ever be perfect here on earth? No, and the criticisms and attacks may intensify, but Saint Peter says in his letter: *"always be ready to make your defense to anyone who demands from you an accounting for the hope that is in you"*, so we have to be ready. That is why we go to church, why we receive the sacraments, why we try to live the word of God, and try to live a good Christian life, not because we are perfect, but because we know that we are weak, sinful, and because we know that our hope is not our own strength, skill and wisdom, but it is all Jesus Christ. As Christians, we know that without Jesus Christ, we are absolute zeros. That is why we try, and whoever tries also makes mistakes, but Christ is here to lift us up and help us walk with him on the right path.

Whoever thinks that he does not need all these things and can do without Christ and the power of the Holy Spirit, is on the wrong path. This self indulgence and justification extinguishes the fire of the Holy Spirit in them and makes their lives all the more difficult. Let us never allow this to be our case, but rather always strive to be open to the action of the Holy Spirit in our lives. Only then, all our thoughts, words, and deeds will become living testimony that we are true disciples of Jesus Christ, who actively live in the Holy Spirit.

Holy Spirit the Advocate

Monday 6th week of Easter,
May 26

Today's readings:
First Reading: Acts 16: 11-15
Responsorial Psalm: Psalms 149: 1b-2, 3-4, 5-6a and 9b
Alleluia: John 15: 26b, 27a
Gospel: John 15: 26 – 16: 4

In today's Gospel, Jesus announces the coming of the Paraclete. What is a Paraclete? The Greek word *Parakletos* literally means advocate or lawyer. One of these two would be a better translation, because this way we would immediately understand that Jesus sends us an advocate into the great battle, the Advocate who will help us defend the true faith. The Advocate will help us give witness to Christ and will give us strength to never falter.

Even when it becomes difficult, even when we will be hated, the Advocate will be with us, strengthening us, helping us be true to God! Being followers of Christ, the going will get tough, and it will get rough too, but that should not discourage us, rather, as Saint Ignatius of Loyola put it - *this should encourage us that we are doing well, because the words of Christ are being fulfilled in our lives: they will hate you for my name's sake, rejoice and be glad, for your reward is great in heaven.*

Let us always remember to pray for guidance and strength, to flee often to the Holy Spirit and to ask him for all his gifts. Only then, strengthened by Him, will we be able to always bear good witness to Christ and, under his inspiration, to say the right words when necessary. Let our prayer often be: *come, Holy Spirit, come.*

Jesus present through the Holy Spirit

**Tuesday 6th week of Easter,
May 27**

Today's readings:
First Reading: Acts 16: 22-34
Responsorial Psalm: Psalms 138: 1-2ab, 2cde-3, 7c-8
Alleluia: John 16: 7, 13
Gospel: John 16: 5-11

"It is to your advantage that I go away, for if I do not go away, the Counselor will not come to you; but if I go, I will send him to you." Jesus himself says that he must go, so that he may send us the Holy Spirit. Why couldn't he simply stay with us? After all, how great would it be to have Jesus here with us, to defend the faith, to perform miracles, to convince everyone that he is the Messiah and be the face of Christianity everywhere. It would surely be much easier than we have as Christians have it now.

But on the other hand, Jesus accepted everything that belongs to humanity, so that includes time, space, and history. Therefore, as God and man, he could not be here on earth in bodily form as we are forever. But that is why he gives us himself differently, so that we could really have him forever, and that is under the species of bread and wine in the Eucharist. True enough, the Eucharist is also possible only because the Lord Jesus is leaving and sending out his Spirit on the world, so that all people everywhere and at every moment can be in his presence, in a sacramental way.

Saint John Chrysostom says: *we lost paradise, but we gained heaven.* The same can be applied today - Jesus as we knew him two thousand years ago left, but we gained through the Holy Spirit the Lord Jesus forever, in the sacramental bread. Anywhere, anytime and in all of us, his Spirit works and brings into reality the true presence of Jesus Christ. In addition, as we too are partakers in the works of the Holy Spirit, through the power of the Holy Spirit, we ourselves become the hands and feet of Jesus and so can bring his presence to all places and people.

What a powerful and comforting truth - we are never alone, wherever we are we have the Holy Spirit with us, working in us, to surely bring about the goodness of the Kingdom of God. Let us do exactly that, everyday, bring Jesus into every place we go, bring his presence there through the power of the Holy Spirit active in us, and so allow him to truly manifest himself in our world today.

Dynamic love of the Holy Trinity

Wednesday 6th week of Easter,
May 28

Today's readings:
First Reading: Acts 17: 15, 22 – 18: 1
Responsorial Psalm: Psalms 148: 1-2, 11-12, 13, 14
Alleluia: John 14: 16
Gospel: John 16: 12-15

It is said of Saint Augustine that as he was once walking along the shore of the Mediterranean Sea and thinking about the Holy Trinity, he tried to understand it so that he could explain it to the faithful. As he was walking and thinking, he met a little boy who had made a small hole in the sand and with a shell was pouring water from the sea into the hole. Saint Augustine stood by him and asked: *what are you doing?* The boy replied: *I will pour the whole sea into this hole.* Saint Augustine replied: *Well that is impossible, you will not pour the whole sea into this hole.* The boy replied to him: *Neither will you ever understand the mystery of the Holy Trinity with your mind.* And with that the boy disappeared. Saint Augustine realized quickly that he met an angel, with a very clear message from God.

Today we celebrate the feast of the Most Holy Trinity. We celebrate the greatest mystery of our faith, the mystery that we are unable to understand with our own mind and reason, like Saint Augustine, like many before him, and many many after him. Three Divine Persons, in one God - a mystery that leaves one speechless.

Although there are so many examples that attempt to explain the Holy Trinity, each one of them falls short. Not one of them expresses exactly and perfectly the entire mystery of the Holy Trinity. On the other hand, there are some aspects of the Holy Trinity that surely can be explained, because we know them from Jesus and revelation. For example, we know there are different relationships in the Holy Trinity, which do not mix. We have God the Father, who only He of the three is the Father and the Creator. Next we have God the Son, who only He is Jesus Christ, who became man, and is the crucified and resurrected Savior and Redeemer of humanity. Finally we have God the Holy Spirit, who only He is the Spirit of God, who descends on man, gives life, revives, comforts and is our advocate. Different roles, different relationships, but one harmonious and constantly active movement of love between them, yet always one God. it is a truly beautiful image but really, we must always remember that God is always more than we can ever explain or imagine.

Even Saint Augustine, after his experience on the seashore, said his famous: *si comprehendis, non est Deus,* which is Latin for *if you understand, it is not God!* He understood that the Holy Trinity is a mystery *par excellence* and must be left a mystery. We too will never understand this great mystery, but one thing we can do, and that is to participate actively in the constantly dynamic movement of love between the three persons of the

Holy Trinity with our own lives and love.

For us today, to celebrate this feast properly is to live properly. We are to live the life of the Most Holy Trinity, to place ourselves in the presence of God and let ourselves be guided by God. We are to participate in their movement of love by letting ourselves be penetrated by God's love, inner peace and harmony. With our whole lives, let ourselves be guided by God's grace, blessing and love because God is love. This love was manifested in the fact that God sent his Son into the world to redeem us all and break our enmity with God. He came down to us when we were still sinners, and by his death and resurrection he invited us into communion with God, into communion with the Most Holy Trinity, into the communion of love, which is poured out in all of us in our hearts through the Holy Spirit whom we have received. Only in such a community is there fullness of life and eternal life. No doubt, this is a daily challenge for all of us but as Saint Paul says, *"I can do all things in him who strengthens me."*

The Church presents us with this celebration today to celebrate our God. Let us strive to take it outside into the world, so that it doesn't remain only a Church celebration, but a celebration of love and harmony for everyone. As we are deeply moved by the dynamic love of the Most Holy Trinity, may we always and everywhere be everyday more authentic witnesses of God's love, so that with our lives living in the Holy Trinity, slowly but surely we will make this world more beautiful.

Everlasting joy

**Thursday 6th week of Easter,
May 29**

Today's readings:
First Reading: Acts 18: 1-8
Responsorial Psalm: Psalms 98: 1, 2-3ab, 3cd-4
Alleluia: John 14: 18
Gospel: John 16: 16-20

Jesus today tells his disciples very openly that he is going to the Father and that he is leaving them. As we approach the end of the Easter season, this reading appears to be out of place as it is from shortly before Jesus' Passion and death. Why are we reading it now and what can it tell us today?

No doubt, this reading has much to tell us and especially the last part: *"Truly, truly, I say to you, you will weep and lament, but the world will rejoice; you will be sorrowful, but your sorrow will turn into joy."* In this once sentence, we hear from Jesus himself, a short summary of his whole Passion, death and resurrection. It is like a short profession of faith, recalling all that is important and what springs from this redemptive event. Jesus himself tells his disciples and us once again that he will suffer greatly which will climax in his death, and so bring two kinds of reactions to it. On the one hand, those who belong to Christ will lament and weep for Jesus, saddened by his passion and death on the cross. On the other hand, those who do not want to belong to Christ, being the world, will rejoice at his death. They will rejoice because the one who bothered their way of life is gone, is dead, no longer can be a nuisance to them and so they can now live life as they like. Indeed, seeing this joy over the death of Christ brings sorrow for those that love Jesus and follow him. But this sorrow does not last, as it will be turned to joy! And that is why we read this reading today, as the joy that springs from the glorious resurrection of Christ is an everlasting joy! It is a permanent joy that cannot be taken away, it is a joy that is deeply rooted in the resurrection victory of Jesus Christ, it is a joy that will never end.

In the Greek Catholic tradition, the prayer hymn *O light gladsome*, directly expresses this everlasting joy as a result of the resurrection of Christ. The prayer recalls beautifully the deep faith of the Christians in Jerusalem in the 2nd century and demonstrates that truly their *sorrow was turned into joy.* As a symbol of the resurrected and glorious Christ, a perpetually burning lamp was placed into his empty tomb. This hymn was sung as a candle was lit from this perpetually burning lamp in the tomb and brought out ceremoniously to remind everyone that the joy of the resurrection never ends, that the resurrected Christ now shines for all to see and brings everlasting joy to everyone that follows him. What a powerful tradition and even more powerful prayer hymn. May we too experience this everlasting joy springing from the resurrection of Christ each and every day of our lives, and may we too join in praying this beautiful hymn:

O Light gladsome
of the holy glory of the Immortal Father,
the Heavenly, the Holy, the Blessed, O Jesus Christ,
having come upon the setting of the sun,
having seen the light of the evening,
We praise the Father, the Son, and the Holy Spirit: God.
Worthy it is at all times to praise Thee in joyful voices,
O Son of God, Giver of Life, for which the world glorifies Thee.
Amen

Do not be afraid, I am with you

Friday 6th week of Easter,
May 30

Today's readings:
First Reading: Acts 18: 9-18
Responsorial Psalm: Psalms 47: 2-3, 4-5, 6-7
Alleluia: Luke 24: 46, 26
Gospel: John 16: 20-23

For a few days now we have been encouraged by Jesus to have hope, that he would send us the Paraclete and Advocate, who would accompany us and help us in our task to bear witness to Him to all people. So it was for the apostles at that time, since Jesus was not always bodily present as he was before his death and resurrection, everything was new for them and new situations came about.

All the more Saint Paul, who we hear about today from the first reading, who met Christ once on the road to Damascus and since then, everywhere he went, cooperated actively with the Holy Spirit. He bore witness to Christ in Corinth, for almost 2 years, and preached there the Word of God. Paul was a witness to Christ in the fullest sense of the term. Even though he was met with danger and problems - Paul held on his certainty - he held on to Christ. Everything else brings with it the possibility of failure, but not when we are with Christ. In difficult times, just as Christ encourages Paul, *"Do not be afraid, but speak and do not be silent; for I am with you,"* he also says this to us.

Such strong words! Through them, one realizes that even though the Lord is invisible, his Spirit is still active and causes the Word of God to spread whether one likes it or not. Let us join in this missionary work, let us also, not be afraid, just speak and testify to Christ - like Paul - because right then, the Lord Himself is around us and in us.

Bring Christ to our meetings

Saturday, Visitation of the Blessed Virgin Mary Feast, May 31

Today's readings:

First Reading: Zephaniah 3: 14-18a or Romans 12: 9-16
Responsorial Psalm: Isaiah 12: 2-3, 4bcd, 5-6
Alleluia: Luke 1: 45
Gospel: Luke 1: 39-56

Today's feast of the Visitation of the Virgin Mary invites us to a beautiful intimate event, to a lovely meeting between Elizabeth and the Virgin Mary. In addition to this meeting, there is also a second meeting, and that is between Jesus and John the Baptist who are both in the womb of their mothers. We can feel in these meetings a deep devotion to God and great love - the Virgin Mary greets Elizabeth with great joy and respect, and in turn Elizabeth and John, inspired by the Holy Spirit, experience enthusiasm and adoration of the Lord in the womb of the Virgin Mary.

To put oneself into this moment, to be there, to look at it, no doubt it these are very touching and powerful meetings. And as we meditate on this today, we realize how essential, necessary, healing, encouraging and fulfilling it is to meet a person face to face - to experience our joys but also our sorrows together, beside each other.

We know that at that time, there were no instant messaging options, but there was direct face to face communication and when they did it, it truly had weight and authenticity. When they wanted to say something to someone, they couldn't send a text message, but they had to meet directly and talk face to face. In this way, slowly but authentically, they created authentic and intimate relationships, relationships that they could lean on, find strength, encouragement and love in them.

Today, perhaps we have become very virtual, often looking at our phones rather than at our loved one sitting beside us, who also is looking at their phone. Sad, but we are losing that direct contact with one another as authentic communication is fading away. Sure, we meet other people, but how authentic and truly valuable are these meetings? When we meet another, it is as if we don't know how to start, what to say, how to communicate and then we stumble for small talk, comment on the weather, and soon enough there it ends.

For all of us, this feast encourages us to meet others authentically and then truly communicate. Also, it is very important to bring Christ into every one of our meetings because he is the one who will unite us most perfectly - even though we don't meet him today, as Elizabeth and John - nonetheless, he acts, he unites us into one people - one heart, one soul.

At the intercession of the Mother of God, let us pray for ourselves, for our communication with others, so that, like the Virgin Mary, who shared her joy with her relative Elizabeth, we too may be open, communicative - build strong relationships and always bring Jesus Christ into them.

Jesus needs us

Sunday, Ascension of the Lord Solemnity, June 1

Today's readings:
First Reading: Acts 1: 1-11
Responsorial Psalm: Psalms 47: 2-3, 6-7, 8-9
Second Reading: Ephesians 1: 17-23 or Hebrews 9: 24-28; 10: 19-23
Alleluia: Matthew 28: 19a, 20b
Gospel: Luke 24: 46-53

Today we celebrate 40 days after the resurrection of Jesus Christ, the feast of the Ascension of the Lord. It is a great feast in the Church, because it is a great event in the life of the risen Christ. In the first reading we heard about this event - Jesus' last moments on earth. He assures his apostles that they will be equipped with power from above, that he will send them the Holy Spirit and they will bear witness to him to all nations. In the Gospel we hear the same thing - Christ will be proclaimed to everyone and it is they who will begin it, they are his witnesses.

However, even though it is Jesus' celebration, it is also our celebration that invites us to act. This event is beautifully attested to by an old legend that describes Jesus' arrival in heaven just after his ascension. It begins: *the archangel Gabriel welcomes Jesus at the gates of heaven and speaks to him a little worriedly: "Lord, now that you have finished your work on earth - what are your plans to ensure that the Word that you proclaimed will spread throughout the world?" Jesus answered him: "I called simple fishermen to spread the Word that I gave them." "Yes, I know about them" - answered the archangel Gabriel - "but what other plans do you have?" The Lord answered him: "I told Peter and the other disciples about the Kingdom of God. They all heard my words and saw my miracles. I especially encouraged Thomas in his faith when he doubted. They saw me die on the cross, but I did not leave them alone - I have now appeared to them for 40 days - they saw that I live forever and ever." "I know that too, Lord" - answered the Archangel Gabriel, still worried - "but if it should not work out, you certainly have a plan B." Jesus calmly answered him: "I have no other plans, I am counting on them."*

What a powerful statement. Jesus is counting on them, and he is counting on us too. The ascension of the Lord is slowly opening up a new style of life in the Church. Up until now, the main emphasis has been on Jesus, he spoke and led everything. Now, after his ascension, and after the sending of the Holy Spirit - the emphasis will be on us - the Church - led by the Spirit of Jesus, to continue his work so that - as we have heard it twice - we may be his witnesses. We are to be his mouth - spreading his Word everywhere, to be his hands - lifting others from the ground and healing, and to be his heart - loving everyone unconditionally and selflessly.

The Lord Jesus is counting on us! He gives us everything we need to make it through and thus bear good fruit and to be his witnesses to all nations. Let us ask Jesus today for a stronger and firmer faith and may we not be frightened by anything as we are equipped with power from above - the power of the Holy Spirit. May we always stand firm in his power, so that what we have received and what we will yet receive, we will use for the building of the kingdom of God and always and everywhere faithfully and with great love testify to Jesus Christ, our Lord.

Humility in all things

**Monday 7th week of Easter,
June 2**

Today's readings:
First Reading: Acts 19: 1-8
Responsorial Psalm: Psalms 68: 2-3ab, 4-5acd, 6-7ab
Alleluia: Colossians 3: 1
Gospel: John 16: 29-33

In this life, sometimes it is quite difficult to see the good in events, especially in our personal very difficult situations. Or even when something bad happens, how to make the best of it? Or when we have a certain plan and in the end it turns out completely differently. How to stay calm in all of these?

Honestly, It's not easy, but complaining definitely won't help us, nor an attitude of despair. As believers, we must never allow such attitudes to overcome us, we must never allow despair and sadness to creep into our hearts, because they destroy everything, they destroy peace, destroy joy, destroy a positive outlook on life. As believers, through prayer and faithfulness to the Lord, we must believe that God truly takes care of us and will provide all that we need. As Saint Paul tells the Romans, who in Rome also did not have it easy and endured all kinds of suffering, *"all things work together for good for those who love God."* Saint Paul could say this because he himself experienced all kinds of difficult and painful moments, situations where he was left completely at the edge of his strength, and had no one but the Lord as his support. It was there that Jesus strengthened him and through that, he was able to continue fighting the good fight.

How many times does the Lord God allow some difficulty in our lives? No doubt He allows such situations so that he could bring us closer to Him. When something is not right, and we need to figure it out, through trials and tough situations God educates us. The biggest problem in these kinds of situations is when, like today's apostles, we think that we know it all, when we think that we can handle it ourselves, when we think we understand and we don't need Jesus. "Now we know that you know all things, and need none to question you; by this we believe that you came from God." Jesus very quickly put things right: *"Do you now believe?"* In other words: where is your humility? *"The hour is coming, indeed it has come, when you will be scattered, every man to his home, and will leave me alone."*

How important it is to have humility in everything we do, to have God first in our lives and look at every event through His eyes. All of us must strive for this, and in marriage even more so - both the husband and the wife together, as there is a difference walking alone through life, with problems and walking together with Christ. Whoever wants to walk alone, will tread a very painful path, but whoever walks with Christ, with the one who strengthens us so that we can carry the cross that we have, has hope, has strength, has peace. *"I have said this to you, that in me you may have peace. In the world you have tribulation; but be of good cheer, I have overcome the world."* Let us ask for this peace in our lives, for his blessing, for humility in all things, that we may not abandon him in our difficulties, but draw closer to him in our pains and so gain strength and peace from him.

Hold me Lord!

**Tuesday 7th week of Easter,
June 3**

Today's readings:
First Reading: Acts 20: 17-27
Responsorial Psalm: Psalms 68: 10-11, 20-21
Alleluia: John 14: 16
Gospel: John 17: 1-11a

The well known Italian saint Philip Neri used to say: *"Hold me Lord, hold Philip, because at any time he can betray you."* How true of a statement this is and a very realistic one at that. Maybe we would not expect such a statement from a priest, but he was very well aware that as a priest he could do a lot of good, but at the same time, he could also disappoint - he knew that he is weak without Jesus.

No wonder that today the Lord Jesus prays for all of us - for priests, for married couples, for young people, for all those who belong to him. We hear it directly from Christ: *"I am praying for them; I am not praying for the world but for those whom thou hast given me, for they are thine."* How powerful - Christ prays for us. He does so because he knows that we cannot do anything without his help and his grace, as we are not strong enough. Jesus knows that we need him, that we need prayer, that we need the sacraments and living faith, we need it all because only then will we be able to continue his work - to change the world for the better, so that they believe through us.

How beautiful it is to belong to Christ and how much it really asks of us! This means, as Christians, we must be authentic and be set aflame with zeal for Christ! How essential this is as only authentic testimony can truly move hearts, only those whose hearts burn for Christ can also set aflame the hearts of others and so win them for Christ! This however never means that we can say we are invincible, but quite the contrary, we too like Saint Philip Neri must pray often: *"hold me Lord, hold me, for at any time I can betray you."* We are strong with Christ, but never totally immune to failing Him. Christ knows this and that is why he prays for us, and so we too must pray for ourselves, and not only ourselves, but for others too.

Let us ask Jesus today for the strength to always bear authentic testimony, so that our hearts burn with love for Him and so be able to set others aflame for Him as well.

First to serve

Wednesday 7th week of Easter, June 4

Today's readings:

First Reading: Acts 20: 28-38
Responsorial Psalm: Psalms 68: 29-30, 33-35a, 35bc-36ab
Alleluia: John 17: 17b, 17a
Gospel: John 17: 11b-19

Today, both the first reading and the Gospel have a similar idea: service. In the Gospel, Jesus prays for his disciples to be strong in their faith and to remain faithful to God in their missionary work. In the first reading, Saint Paul also encourages his believers not to be discouraged by the various attacks that will come, but to remain faithful to God and conscientiously care for the flock entrusted to them.

We see that both Jesus and Saint Paul encourage us to serve faithfully. This also applies to us today, we too must remain faithful to God, so that what we have received from Him we do not throw away when difficult times come. Even when we do not see the fruit of our labor right away, we must believe that the fruit will come, we just need to serve faithfully and persistently.

This is why both Jesus and Saint Paul encourage us to serve, because they know that without encouragement often, the motivation to serve may become quite low. They both encourage us through today's Word to bring our hopes up and motivate us that true service brings great rewards. However, they also are aware of the danger of the evil one, who is always lurking and who wants to disgust us, wants us to despair, wants us to be lazy and be indifferent to others. This is a typical tactic of the evil one - to bring about that we do not pray, do not draw strength from the Lord, that we do not want to serve, do not want to sacrifice, do not want to go the extra mile. The evil one constantly pushes us to look for excuses why we cannot help and of course, there is always the easier way, where I do not see, I do not care, I have my own peace. However, we all know from Scripture, that easy path is the meritless path and ends up bringing loneliness and sadness.

Saint Paul reminds us in the first reading, that *"it is more blessed to give than to receive"*, which we can also understand as it is more blessed to serve than to be served, it is more blessed to give oneself, than to keep everything selfishly.

Today, we pray for the gift of willingness to serve others, for the spirit of service. Let us never wait on others to serve us, but always be the first ones to serve them out of love because we want to follow Christ as best we can. Doing so, we will imitate our Lord in humble service and not only that, but also be abundantly blessed with great rewards from God.

Stand firm in the Truth!

Thursday, Boniface, Bishop, Martyr, June 5

Today's readings:
First Reading: Acts 22: 30; 23: 6-11
Responsorial Psalm: Psalms 16: 1-2a and 5, 7-8, 9-10, 11
Alleluia: John 17: 21
Gospel: John 17: 20-26

Today the Church celebrates Saint Boniface of Germany. An interesting fact from my hometown Winnipeg, where I grew up, is that the city is split into two Roman Catholic dioceses - Winnipeg Archdiocese and Saint Boniface Archdiocese. It is not very common for a city to have two Roman Catholic dioceses and even less so, for one of them to be named after a saint. Almost always the diocese bears the name of the city, but in Winnipeg it is like this, because it is the result of the joining of two cities - the English city Winnipeg and the French city Saint Boniface. As the cities grew, they merged, but because of pastoral and cultural difficulties between the English and French, the Vatican created two archdioceses to resolve the problem - the English Archdiocese of Winnipeg and the French

Archdiocese of Saint Boniface.

Why say all this? Today as we celebrate Saint Boniface, we remember a great bishop who worked in the 8th century in what is now Germany, proclaimed the Word of God and fiercely fought against local pagan customs. At that time in that region, many Christians were turning back to superstition, witchcraft and offering sacrifices to idols. He is known for his deep devotion to the faith, but also for his great courageous deed which occurred in the town of Fritzlar. There, the people considered a large oak tree dedicated to the pagan god of thunder to be the main place of sacrifice. Boniface knew that this was bad, so he decided that he would cut it down. The people waited with horror at what would happen - that he would be struck by lightning by the pagan god, but of course, nothing like that happened. When thc people saw that their pagan god had proven powerless against Boniface, they repented and re-accepted the faith. Boniface then also built the chapel of Saint Peter from the wood of this cut down tree. Soon, the faith spread in Germany and continued to grow. It was also met with the enthusiasm of the great German rulers. Even at the age of 80, Boniface's missionary zeal and love for Christ did not leave him and he continued to visit the very first places of his work for Christ. However, that is where he met his death. Near the city of Dokkum, he was ambushed by a group of fanatical pagans, who murdered both him and his entire group of fifty companions. After his martyrdom, he was immediately revered by the local believers as a great saint.

What can we take from all of this? As was then, so also today, a certain form of paganism is pressing upon us from every side, which is mainly the culture of death. It may seem quite attractive and many allow themselves to accept it, but as they do so, they abandon Christ and serve the evil powers within them. Like Saint Boniface, we too must face these dangers and defend ourselves, fight for the truth, fight for Christ. No doubt, evil has many forms and appearances, which is exactly why Christ again prays for us today in the Gospel: *"I have given them thy word; and the world has hated them because they are not of the world, even as I am not of the world. I do not pray that thou shouldst take them out of the world, but that thou shouldst keep them from the evil one. They are not of the world, even as I am not of the world. Sanctify them in the truth; thy word is truth."*

We clearly see that victory is on the side of Truth - Christ is the Truth. Everyone who belongs to Christ, who serves Him, gives Him their lives - are victors - like Saint Boniface long ago. Like him, we too are not to be of this world and accept the evil this world offers, but live in the truth of Christ, even at those times when it seems very difficult. May we never be deceived by the wickedness and falsehood of this world, but let us stand firm in Christ! In Him, we will be sanctified already here on Earth, and by showing Him that we too are true to Him, He will surely give us His victory and not only here on earth, but more importantly in the next age, with Him in heaven.

Do you agapas me?

**Friday 7th week of Easter,
June 6**

Today's readings:
First Reading: Acts 25: 13b-21
Responsorial Psalm: Psalms 103: 1-2, 11-12, 19-20ab
Alleluia: John 14: 26
Gospel: John 21: 15-19

Today, we have heard one of the most beautiful conversations, if not the most beautiful conversation in the New Testament. It is the conversation between the resurrected Jesus and Peter. It is an intimate conversation, conducted by Jesus, focused only on Peter, and with the aim of finding out one essential thing: whether Peter really loves him.

Let us remember that originally Peter was called Simon, but Jesus specially chose him to be the rock, Cephas (Hebrew), Petros (Latin), so that he would be the Rock on whom Jesus would build his Church. This of course brings great responsibility. Christ asks of him stability and firmness - but, as we hear today, Peter is not to be firm because of his own strength, not "I myself, I can do it," but firm because of deep sincere love for Christ.

And so, since Peter denied Jesus during his passion three times, Jesus now wants to know how much Peter loves him, whether he is serious and whether he wants to be that rock or not. He does not reproach him for anything, does not expose his mistake, but calmly asks about his love for him.

What is interesting, is that Jesus uses Peter's original name Simon: *"Simon, do you love me?"* Jesus uses "Simon" to remind Peter where he once was and to help him realize where he can be if he follows Him! (As an important side note, English does not have as many words for "love" as Greek does and so we lose a little bit of the play on words in this text, but sure enough it can still be demonstrated with the Greek words for love.) Therefore, to make it easier to understand, we will use the Greek words instead. So, returning back to the first question, it stands: *"Simon, do you agapas me more than these?" Agapas* is the Greek word for the highest form of love, it is sacrificing love, love that gives everything. Essentially, Jesus is asking Peter if he loves him so much to even give his life for him. Peter however, very aware of his three denials not too long ago, answers Jesus very humbly: *"yes Lord, I filo you." Filo* is the Greek word for love at a friendship level, so Peter's answer could translate to *I care for you* or *I like you*. Jesus sees Peter's sincerity and gives him the task: *"Feed (Greek: boske) my lambs (Greek: arnia)."*

Jesus asks him a second time: *"Simon, do you agapas me?"* Peter again answers as before, with humility: *"Lord, I filo you."* Jesus sees that Peter is no longer full of pride as he was before, but is truly humble and realizes he is weak without Jesus. Peter now receives another task: *"Shepherd (Greek: poimaine) my sheep (Greek: probata)."*

Jesus asks Peter a third time, but this time he changes his word for love to how Peter was answering him: *"Simon, do you filo me?"* Peter is now totally and completely humbled, he answers: *"Lord, you know everything, you know that I filo you."* Peter realizes that he is totally dependent on Christ, no longer "I can do it alone", but humble dependence on the Master, on Jesus, without whom he can do nothing. Jesus gives him a third task: *"Feed (Greek: boske) my sheep (Greek: probata)."*

Each time, Jesus gives Peter a task based on his love. Taken all into account, Peter's task is to be a good and caring shepherd of God's people. Peter in his answers showed Jesus that he truly loves Him, even though he knows that it is not *agape* but only *filio.* Peter gives Jesus everything he has and hands over to Jesus the rest, hoping and believing that He will complete it with his grace. And Jesus does exactly that! Because of his honesty and humility, Jesus can work wonders in him and eventually does bring Peter's love to the highest level, to *agape,* when Peter is crucified upside down in Rome out of love for Christ.

What a powerful and deep conversation of love. It is no different for us! The Lord also asks us, every day and at every moment: *"Do you agapas me?"* Our answer should be similar to Peter's: *Lord, it is not always 100%, but help me to always love you more.* Let us not rely on our own strength and wit, that is exactly why Peter fell and denied Christ three times during his Passion. But let us be like Peter today, let us hold on to Christ and be dependent on him, so that our weaknesses do not rule in us, but the power of Christ, springing from our sincere and humble love for him.

Stay focused! Eyes on Christ!

Saturday 7th week of Easter,
June 7

Today's readings:
First Reading: Acts 28: 16-20, 30-31
Responsorial Psalm: Psalms 11: 4, 5 and 7
Alleluia: John 16: 7, 13
Gospel: John 21: 20-25

How often do we get distracted? Sometimes it looks like we're perpetually distracted by something around us. We have our phones, the TV, and even computers are constantly trying to suck us in and bring our attention to them. They are definitely helpful in our everyday tasks, but sometimes they can be too much for us and really take us away from what is more important. In many ways, the same is true for us as Christians in our prayer life and in our faith in general. Here too, we can get distracted. So often we let the little things of our faith distract us from what's truly important, we nitpick and so lose from sight what is truly essential and needed.

We see something similar in the Gospel today. Peter asks Jesus about John: *"Lord, what about this man?"* What an interesting question by Peter, especially because just moments before this, Jesus asks Peter about his love for him. Peter is distracted by the fate of others, takes his eyes off the goal, but is quickly brought back to reality by Jesus: *"what is that to you? Follow me!"* Jesus wants Peter to focus on what is important and to do what he expects from him - to follow him regardless of what will be with others or what others will do. Truly, this also applies to us, as there is no need to be so curious about others, as they are not our responsibility or concern, we are first and foremost supposed to follow Jesus. We are to give all our attention to following Jesus as best we can and not get distracted by others or events. True to say, this is the second time Jesus tells this to Peter. The first time was at the beginning of his ministry, when Jesus was walking on water and Peter wished to come to him on the water. He is told to do so by Jesus and so Peter got out of the boat and walked on the water to Jesus. Everything was going fine as long as Peter had his eyes on Jesus, but as soon as he was distracted by the waves, he began to sink. Jesus tells him that he had little faith, or in other words, was distracted by what was around him and did not focus on Jesus.

How important it is for us to keep our eyes on Jesus, to focus on him and put all our strength into following him as best we can. The distractions will always be there, we are to ignore them and focus. Let us pray today to remain focused on our path in following Jesus and so never risk sinking into distractions that would only lead us far from Christ.

Engraved into our hearts

Sunday, Pentecost Solemnity, June 8

Today's readings:

First Reading: Acts 2: 1-11

Responsorial Psalm: Psalms 104: 1, 24, 29-30, 31, 34

Second Reading: First Corinthians 12: 3b-7, 12-13 or Romans 8: 8-17

Gospel: John 20: 19-23 or John 14: 15-16, 23b-26

Pentecost! Today we celebrate the sending of the Holy Spirit. This event marks the definitive beginning of our Church and of our faith. From this event, it became clear to the apostles that they no longer professed the Jewish faith, but professed the fulfillment of the Jewish faith - Jesus Christ resurrected. Today all doubts have been definitively dispelled for them as they received the Holy Spirit, the power from above, so that they could zealously bear witness to Christ to all people.

We all know about this event, of the Descent of the Holy Spirit. We heard about it in the first reading, how on the 50th day after the Jewish Passover and also the 50th day after Christ's resurrection - the apostles were locked in a room and waited praying. They did so, because they received the command from the resurrected Christ at his ascension, not to leave Jerusalem, as they were yet to receive power from above. Their waiting reminds us of the waiting of Moses and the Israelites under Mount Sinai, also on the 50th day after the exodus from Egypt, after the Passover. Just as long ago under Mount Sinai, when the Spirit of God descended in fire and engraved God's law on stone, today, on the 50th day, the Spirit of God descends in fire and engraved Himself in the hearts of the apostles. It is no longer God's law on stone, but it is better, it is its fulfillment - it is God Himself, He is that same power from Mount Sinai, but this time the Holy Spirit gives Himself to all of us in a special way: He engraves Himself into our hearts.

Let us note that as soon as the Holy Spirit descended on the apostles, all obstacles that they seemed to have disappeared. Every fear, uncertainties, doubts, feelings of weakness and inadequacy - everything such thing is destroyed by the power of the Holy Spirit. The apostles are truly strengthened by power from above, strengthened by the Holy Spirit and his power is perfectly manifested in their lives - they testify of Christ with full power and zeal.

This also applies to us today, in our lives! The Holy Spirit and his power, his presence, enables us to handle everything that we ourselves would not have been able to handle or accomplish. Just as the apostles were able to testify of Christ only by his power, so too, only in the Holy Spirit, are we able to say *"Jesus Christ is Lord."* Only in the Holy Spirit, can our lives have stability, gain direction, certainty, and truly have meaning.

How important is it for us as well to ask for this power from above. Only when we leave room for the Holy Spirit in our lives, only when we open our hearts to Him, will He be able to fully manifest and realize Himself in us. Only when we ourselves experience the descent of the Holy Spirit on us, engraved into our hearts, will things in our lives begin to change for the better. From that moment, we will no longer walk this life alone, but the Holy Spirit will accompany us with His grace and power. May this celebration become especially our celebration, so that we may fully experience His blessing and reap its fruit of love, joy, and peace abundantly.

About the Author

Born and raised in Winnipeg, Canada, in a very multicultural society. Later I moved to Europe and received my Masters in Philosophy and Theology.

Now I enjoy spending time with my family and daughter.

Also by Mathias Gocik

Adam, where are you?
Spiritual Exercises and Meditative Adorations

Grow in love towards God with *Adam, where are you?* and explore the beauty of God's Word.

This book is divided into two parts: spiritual exercises and meditative adorations.

The first part, spiritual exercises are two separate meditations that deal with topics close to my own life experience. The first one called "Adam, where are you?" is a longer and therefore also a deeper spiritual exercise. It reflects my experience of getting lost in life and in my spiritual life as well, and then experiencing God ever searching for me and inviting me to know him through his Word. The second renewal is shorter, and is called "Teach us to pray", which deals with exactly that idea. Prayer may be at times quite difficult and so this renewal can be taken to revive our own prayer life.

The second part of the book are seven meditative adorations, written to accompany the reader on various subjects and occasions. They span from the first being connected to the spiritual exercises "Adam, where are you?", to life discernment, to an adoration for Lent, Advent and a few other occasions.

Salvation is for Everyone
A philosophical and theological analysis of the Anonymous Christian theory by Karl Rahner

The objective of *Salvation is for Everyone* is to present as clearly as possible the *anonymous Christian theory* as portrayed by Karl Rahner. This requires exploring his philosophy, which creates the basis for his theology and then exploring his theology directly regarding the topic.

Principally, this book may be beneficial to Christians, in the sense that they come to understand the real possibility of salvation for non-Christians, as was accepted by the Second Vatican Council. Also, because of the universality of God's salvific will and the universal redemptive saving power of the death and resurrection of Jesus Christ, salvation is a possibility and is attainable even for those outside explicit Christianity, especially for those who live good virtuous lives and strive to follow their conscience. Karl Rahner calls them Anonymous Christians.

Manufactured by Amazon.ca
Acheson, AB

33563005R00074